THE COLLABORATIVE
SOCIAL STUDIES CLASSROOM

THE COLLABORATIVE SOCIAL STUDIES CLASSROOM

A Resource for Teachers, Grades 7–12

Joseph John Nowicki

Kerry F. Meehan

Allyn & Bacon
Boston London Toronto Sydney Tokyo Singapore

Series Editor: Virginia Lanigan
Editorial Assistant: Nihad Farooq
Marketing Manager: Kathleen Hunter
Production Administrator: Susan McIntyre
Editorial-Production Service: Ruttle, Shaw & Wetherill Inc.
Cover Administrator: Suzanne Harbison
Composition Buyer: Linda Cox
Manufacturing Buyer: Aloka Rathnam

Copyright © 1996 by Allyn & Bacon
A Simon & Schuster Company
Needham Heights, Mass. 02194

Library of Congress Cataloging-in-Publication Data

Nowicki, Joseph John.
    The collaborative social studies classroom : a resource for teachers /
Joseph John Nowicki, Kerry F. Meehan.
        p.   cm.
    Includes bibliographic references and index.
    ISBN 0-205-17391-8
    1. Social sciences—Study and teaching (Elementary)—United
States.   2. Social sciences—Study and teaching (Secondary)—United
States.   3. Social sciences—United States—Curricula.   I. Meehan,
Kerry F.   II. Title.
LB1584.N68   1996
370'.71—dc20   95-13741
                                                CIP

Printed in the United States of America
10 9 8 7 6 5 4 3 2 1   00 99 98 97 96 95

To
Kathy and Donna

Contents

Preface

This is a book for teachers written by two teachers who thoroughly enjoy teaching social studies. Our purpose in writing this book is twofold. The first is to share with other teachers four basic strategies that emphasize student-centered and activity-based instruction. The second is to offer teachers a model to create comprehensive lessons using the three components that we include in every lesson we teach: *factual knowledge, skill development,* and *conceptual knowledge.* These basic ingredients for designing activity-centered classrooms infuse every lesson with an effective blend of knowledge acquisition and student ownership while providing motivation for student learning. We believe an understanding of these areas will help all teachers develop the type of lessons that bring classrooms alive.

Between us, we share more than forty years of educational experience in grades 7 through 12. We have experienced teaching from the perspectives of an administrator and a special needs educator and both of us have taught social studies *and* English classes.

This book reflects a desire to share our strategies, lesson designs, and activities with other teachers interested in developing restructured and cooperative classrooms. In recent years many teachers, both visitors to our school and colleagues hearing of our experiences at workshops, have asked, "How do you teach social studies in a heterogeneous classroom?" There is no simple answer. There is no magic formula or mechanistic model of teaching. But there are approaches, many highlighted in this book, that we find work for *all* our students. In addition to these approaches, we offer a *perspective* on course content, design, and methodology to support and guide teachers looking to change. If there is anything we have learned about teaching, it is that teachers do not want to be stagnant. However, teachers who want change need support from their peers and help from the system. They cannot do it alone.

Reconfiguration in the classroom means restructuring in the school. Teachers must take ownership in that restructuring as well as in the redesign of curriculum and the methodology to deliver that curriculum. We both agree that if we were forced to follow a routine and a methodology imposed by others, we would not be teaching.

However, every one of us, by using the power of the teaching profession, can create, innovate, and implement. The need to try something new and different is part of teaching. It is reflected in the thousands of lessons developed during a teaching career. Unfortunately teachers often find themselves isolated from others in the profession. When a teacher retires after twenty-five or thirty years in the profession, a wealth of strategies and insights may also leave the profession. We recognize that one major obstacle to sharing is that teachers do not have enough time to develop and refine approaches collaboratively with their peers. They don't have the time to *professionally brainstorm*. We hope this book provides some relief to teachers looking for help in developing their teaching strategies and allows them to begin a dialogue with their colleagues. It is a book that "kicks around some ideas" and shares some of our products.

The book begins with a short overview describing the roots of our strategies in a research and theoretical base. Any set of models or strategies must have a basis and be grounded in sound educational theory. Yet theory needs to be adapted by those who practice the art of teaching and work every day in a classroom.

The second chapter focuses on the three components of learning we see as universal to all lessons. These elements, *factual knowledge, skill development,* and *conceptual knowledge,* remain in focus throughout the rest of the book. The second chapter also introduces the four families of specific strategies presented in greater detail in the following chapters. Chapter 2 offers our rationale for designing, building, and evaluating cooperative lessons. Our activities are designed for classrooms that are not grouped by gender, socioeconomic, or ethnic background, culture, or ability. *These activities are for classrooms that use mixed ability grouping and therefore represent the total diversity of the school.*

Each of the next four chapters begins with an overview of a specific strategy and then presents detailed examples of lessons. We offer more than one hundred lessons. Our strategies reflect the diversity found in the scope and sequence of any social studies curriculum for grades six through twelve. Although many of the activities favor secondary classrooms, the strategies can be generalized, modified, or reconstructed to fit many course and grade levels. As we repeatedly point out in the examples, teachers can use exactly what we offer or modify to fit their needs. We also provide an appendix including samples of all forms we use.

Chapters 2 through 6 also offer strategies that build on one another. For example, the *Interview Strategies* in Chapter 3 involve one level of learning, and the *Demonstration Strategies* in Chapter 4 work at a higher order. Both the *Trial Strategies* in Chapter 5 and the *Theory Building Strategies* in Chapter 6 expand and incorporate the learning of the previous chapters. In this way a teacher can choose to intertwine the separate groups of strategies in one large project or simply use a particular strategy as the basis for a distinct lesson.

We are sure that what we present can be applied by any social studies teacher to a specific classroom. We see these strategies as high-interest activities that integrate the material of the social studies with the real world students encounter. We recognize the importance of the students' intellectual constructs both individually and collectively. Our emphasis is on cooperative learning and skill development as well as on student accountability and responsibility.

In closing, we offer you these insights and observations in the hope that, as fellow teachers, you share our desire to improve what we do as teachers. As teachers we share the burdens; now let us share the creativity.

CHAPTER 1

An Introduction

Nearly eight years ago our faculty and school adopted a policy that promoted heterogeneous groups and abolished our former system of tracked groups of students. As we began rewriting our curricula, we discovered that our problems were often in the presentation of material, the activities, and the strategies. At times students seemed disconnected from the academic side of their lives and intellectually battered. Although students were willing to go along with their teachers, they did not have any stake in what they were doing, and for some students, learning had no meaning.

Many things in a student's life "turn them off" to school and foster their alienation from the academic world. Complex societal issues that were inconceivable twenty years ago confront students and teachers today. Consequently we must devise strategies to reach out to all the diverse groups of students who inhabit the schools of the nineties. As teachers we must continue to find ways for students to invest their interests in learning and to connect what we teach to their world.

This book presents more than one hundred teaching strategies and activities for use in middle and secondary schools that are designed to encompass all students. Their focus is to help students develop a sense of ownership over their ideas and an awareness of how they analyze and apply the ideas of others. Many of these strategies build on the ideas of Piaget (1969), stressing the role of learner as "a young researcher, busily exploring the environment and constructing schemata" (Phillips & Soltis, 1991, p. 51). At the core are topics that fall under the category of social studies, though many of these easily traverse boundaries between subject areas. Rather than limiting our perspective to a single content area, we focus on the process of teaching through universally applied strategies.

By sharing these instructional strategies with other educators we hope to demonstrate the importance of the art of teaching. Classrooms should be places of intellectual activity and excitement. One way to breathe energy into a classroom is to integrate a student's learning with a student's life. To this end, the strategies and activities we outline in this work serve as an educational and intellectual bridge between the wealth of content material and the everyday world.

What we learn, how we learn, and how it affects our lives depends on how we recognize, analyze, apply, and synthesize what is presented to us. Each of us carries around definitions of the world. We all have positions that we develop to varying degrees of complexity. These positions are our way of understanding and identifying who we are. They come from what we observe, what is presented to us, and what we choose to investigate. Our personal definitions of what is around us form intellectual frameworks. Because these frameworks are not separate from the material we teach in our classrooms, we should not divide the intellectual world from the real world in our classrooms. We need to take a moment to examine our content and methodology. As John Solas advises, "there is perhaps no process more fundamentally important in one's thinking about education than the teaching-learning process." (1992, p. 205)

THE PLAN OF THE BOOK

In devising this book we decided to stress two important areas in constructing a lesson that actively involves and meets the needs of all students. The first is a collection of strategies and activities from our work in many classrooms and with hundreds of students from suburban to rural school districts. These strategies and activities represent patterns of practice that can be directly integrated into classroom teaching. Although not thematic in terms of curriculum content, these strategies do offer themes for classroom teaching. Additionally, each set of strategies is further organized into time frames, creating lessons for a day, a week, or a unit. Some of the activities are designed to act as lessons on their own, and others can be used to supplement an existing curriculum.

The second emphasis specifically identifies the three components of every lesson that integrate the different types of knowledge and skills addressed in social studies classrooms. These lessons pay particular attention to the discovery, construction, and synthesis of knowledge.

SHARING EXPERIENCES FROM THE CLASSROOM

Active and creative teachers are an essential element in the process of education. This book will stimulate dialogue among these teachers as well as reflection by individual teachers. Individual teachers can reinterpret the strategies of learning we offer for use in their own classrooms. Teaching is an interpersonal activity that depends on the personal knowledge teachers acquire and use. Our intent is to provide a forum for sharing ideas and strategies that can be modified and used by the professional community.

APPROACHES TO LEARNING
FROM A TEACHER'S POINT OF VIEW

Teachers, for the most part, are organized and efficient individuals. They have expectations that are based on sets of plans ranging in time from a class, to a day, week, quarter, semester, or year. Many teachers at the senior high school select and teach topics that reflect their own intellectual interests. Many secondary social studies teachers, however, work in a situation far from the ideal they saw during their college preparation. Some teachers wish to imitate their mentors. Other teachers expect their students to share their interest in a subject area. Others expect the same sense of respect for the subject that is found in a college classroom. However, learning today must be based on the curiosity of the individual student, not on the teachers' interests.

As teachers our focus must center on developing the student's natural curiosity and channeling it to topics in the social studies classroom. We must include all students as active participants in their learning. We can then become guides who nurture students' inherent curiosity while directing it to events and ideas of the past. Yet we cannot stop there. We must continue to establish a process that leads students through a taxonomy (such as that of Bloom et al., 1956). Students need to apply their ideas to gain a synthesis that fosters an understanding of their past and present as the foundation for their future.

APPROACHES TO LEARNING EMPHASIZING STUDENTS' INVOLVEMENT

Over our careers as teachers, many of us have agonized about the class that simply stares back without response. We have tried to find ways of cracking the hard veneer of those uninvolved students. Considering that we are probably dealing with more than one hundred students in a day, this is not an easy task. Still, the knowledge that even one person remains uninvolved, and at times hostile to our efforts, hurts even the most battle-scarred teacher.

Consequently, it is time to strike the overused word *motivation* from our collective vocabularies. Motivation speaks about a one-sided effort; "Teachers must motivate"; "Students must become self-motivators." Whether we enjoy the mechanics of the Congress of Vienna or of life in ancient Egypt is not the issue. Motivating students means we are required to make them excited about the Congress of Vienna or life in ancient Egypt. This goal is not a valid assumption.

In the typical year-long ninth grade world history class, it is impossible to motivate all students to respond to every topic found in a world history curriculum. The problem with "motivational" thinking is that it puts the onus on the teacher to motivate or to create the self-motivator. A better word to address what must take place in social studies classes is the word *involve*.

Involvement enhances the individual's ownership of knowledge, creativity, and behavior. Involvement encourages inherent curiosity. Students need to feel involved in the process of learning. Students must operate in a shared and cooperative setting to react to each other and gradually through this involvement, this ownership, gain knowledge. As Dewey (1958) stated:

Through social intercourse, through sharing in the activities embodying beliefs, he (the student) gradually acquires a mind of his own. The conception of mind as a purely isolated possession of the self if at the very antipodes of the truth . . . the self is not a separate mind building up knowledge anew on its own account. (p. 344)

At the same time we must recognize that there are obstacles to involving students in their learning. There are issues that need to be clarified and dealt with to allow students to exercise their intellectual curiosity.

One obstacle is the fear of not completing the course of studies as dictated by the curriculum that drives much of traditional social studies education. An examination of the litany of topics and the time allotted to cover them is staggering: The Mexican War—one week, the Reformation—four days, World War II—two weeks, Ancient Greece—one week. This scheduling emphasizes a fact-based curriculum that places tremendous demands on the student's ability to memorize by rote. However to involve students, and in the words of Dewey to "share activities" and acquire "a mind of his own," requires that students no longer deal only with facts. Now we must stress activities that emphasize how to research, analyze, apply, and synthesize ideas.

As social studies teachers we must constantly reflect on a perspective that equates the past to the present and projects to a viable future. We teach social studies subjects because social studies are not simply names, dates, and capitals. To us, social studies comprises a set of ideas that are intriguing and important because they hold the history, the insight, and the knowledge of who we are as a society and as individuals. It is both personal and interpersonal. Consequently, social studies is alive because it represents constructs created by humans. Solas supports this involvement view of educating:

If teachers and students have been previously approached as information processors in need of direction, they are now being conceptualized as sense-making and history-making deconstructionists, endowed with the ability to reject, describe, and discuss their thoughts, feelings, and actions. (1992, p. 220)

Many of the strategies in the second part of this book are structured to help students discover the meaning behind the facts. These strategies act as a guide and offer suggestions to involve students in their own learning. They place students in activities that foster their abilities to "reject, describe, and discuss their thoughts, feelings, and actions" (Solas, 1992, p. 220).

APPLYING SOCIAL STUDIES LEARNING TO LATER LIFE EXPERIENCES

The true value of social studies is its basis of lifelong learning. Aside from specific dates and times, social studies provide a conceptual framework for understanding our lives. As an example, think about how we can gain the knowledge and respect for the cultural diversity inherent in the world, a nation, or a town. We can see either the insignificance or the importance of a single life or society in the course of time. Social studies give us a perspective of how we have made decisions in the past and how we should make them in the future. It is no wonder that the discussions of the ancients about issues such as life, truth, goodness, war, peace, government, and social life are as pertinent today as they were then. As educators, we should think about Phillips and Soltis's (1991) comment, "Dewey did not deny that human learners can be given information by their teachers. But, unless the learner had struggled personally with an issue, the information was likely to be committed to memory in a rather lifeless or mechanical way" (p. 39).

Social studies should offer us the opportunity to "struggle personally with an issue" and develop explanations about who we are, why we are, and how to address issues of equality, inhumanity, discrimination, and justice. Social studies are not simply left in the empty classroom when summer vacation begins or locked away when the book is closed. These issues surround us every day in everything we encounter. Our task is to help students learn to integrate this knowledge.

THE IMPORTANCE OF INTEGRATING KNOWLEDGE

In developing any curriculum there are two important areas that teachers must address. First, the knowledge base must not be limited to a single source of truth. Second, it is essential to recognize that learning includes the social experiences we share. These experiences give us the humanity through which we construct our truths. Social studies are the study of those collective experiences.

Any curriculum in the social studies must not only include our social experiences as a component of study but must also foster student thinking in a reflective process linking the material from the classroom with the experience of social life. In this approach, the student applies the raw material that is at the core of a particular subject area to his or her own experiences and relative to the experiences of others. In this manner the student begins to create individual conclusions. This reflective experience is spawned from student-generated ideas and creates a knowledge base the student owns. At the same time that knowledge base can be applied and shared with others in the common dialogue of a classroom.

Integrating life experiences with academic curriculum encourages diversity and curiosity (see for example Ekland Shoemaker, 1989; Taba, 1967; Joyce & Weil, 1980). Sharing the knowledge they have constructed with others stimulates student dialogue and enhances the development of critical thinking skills. Integrating classroom material with the realities of external life experiences involves students in their learning as they begin to construct new meanings. The ideas students create through their own reflection and curiosity carry significance because students have a greater stake in what they learn. The sharing of ideas reflects the process of social exchange and becomes a part of students' everyday life.

SOCIAL STUDIES AS A SERIES OF IDEAS

Social studies are essentially a series of fluid and dynamic ideas. Students need not be at some highly abstract level to understand this. Nearly all junior or senior high school students can handle this notion once they discover the process of creating their own ideas as well as understanding and recognizing the origin of these ideas. At the same time, what we teach, how we teach, and how we evaluate student success often lags far behind the recognition of ideas as a basis of student learning. For example, if teachers continually define the knowledge to be learned, as well as the methodology students may use to gain that knowledge, then teachers are overmanaging the process. This limits, rather that releases, the energy and potential of learners creating their own knowledge base. Ideas can become the battle ground as they have through history in any academic or social setting. Control of ideas keeps the school from becoming such a battle ground and stifles both creative thought and the development of a student-centered learning process.

CONSTRUCTING A PERSONAL KNOWLEDGE OF THE SOCIAL WORLD FROM THE SOCIAL STUDIES CLASSROOM

The challenge to social studies education is that students build on the information from the classroom and synthesize this learning into their lives. There is a powerful history of such an approach in educational philosophy suggested by both Dewey and Piaget, among others. The theoretical framework goes beyond the realm of educational thought and includes the work of many philosophers and social scientists, such as Dewey's colleague George Herbert Mead (1932) and Berger and Luckman (1967). For the classroom teacher, this means that students need to personally reconstruct the realities presented through social studies if they are to analyze, interpret, understand, and apply them. This is undeniably a social process.

One result of this synthesis is that students begin to form their own conclusions and develop their own insights as problem solvers. Students begin to engage in a dialogue and a debate. Students shape their own knowledge. They create a base of awareness that stays with them because it is their own, and thus it has a greater sense of meaning. Ultimately, this foundation of knowledge has been produced by the student. His or her personalized mark is on it.

Social studies education should enable students to complete this process of integrating the curriculum into their window on everyday life. It is the teacher's responsibility to develop the strategies and activities that foster student involvement in learning. The strategies and activities that follow in later chapters are designed to help teachers accomplish this.

THE COOPERATIVE CLASSROOM

Learning is not a solitary activity. Education involves a great many people sharing ideas over time. Why then, are our classrooms and learning experiences often structured to separate people and keep them from working together? Social life is dependent on others. When society breaks down it is because people choose not to work together. Yet many social studies classrooms seek to keep people apart. This enforced separation may be due in part to the belief that intense individual competition is necessary for producing the best minds or to the assertion that competition is the only way to prepare students for a life in which there will never be enough resources to satisfy everyone's desires. Or competition may be viewed as a mechanism of control educators use to manage classrooms and to keep the focus on a single agenda.

As educators we are not opposed to competition. There are numerous opportunities in our strategies and activities for healthy competition among groups or teams, between individuals, and most importantly, with oneself. Through these experiences individuals grow intellectually, emotionally, and physically. Competition in the social studies classroom is healthy when it encourages cooperation. It should serve to involve individuals in a common dialogue and effort rather than to separate them.

The cooperative classroom is one in which people work with instead of against one another. It reflects the world outside of school, where often problems are solved through community efforts. Also it is a place in which students are responsible for and accountable to themselves and to peers.

Cooperative learning strategies, like the constructivist orientation toward teaching and learning, are not an overnight happening devoid of a professional history. There is a growing body of literature supporting efforts at bringing cooperation and collaboration to the classroom. The works of Johnson and Johnson (1975), Slavin (1980, 1983), Kagan (1990), and Tyrrel (1990) offer strong endorsement and guidelines for such activities.

In this book we frequently use terms such as cooperative work, collaborative work, the cooperative classroom, and working together. We see each of these terms related to the definitions identified in the literature as cooperative learning. Cooperative learning has been identified in models presented by Robert Slavin (1989, 1990) and Johnson and Johnson (1975), among others. Their models are specific in organizing explicit roles for students to follow in classroom settings. Although our strategies include roles for students to follow, the roles are classroom specific. Our strategies do not follow the models of cooperative learning exactly. They assign roles to students in cooperative and collaborative settings, yet suggest roles that can be created by students and classroom teachers engaged in similar endeavors.

This is not to detract from existing models of cooperative learning. We celebrate their goals. These models have served as invaluable guides to many teachers engaged in adapting cooperative work strategies to mixed-ability classrooms. Our strategies may be considered an expanding of the existing cooperative learning models. Although this work presents a model for analyzing lessons, it does not present a new model for encouraging collaboration within classrooms. In fact, we see our efforts fitting well within various descriptions of cooperative learning. In 1985 Jeannie Oakes suggested:

> Cooperative learning occurs when teachers have students work together in small groups on a task toward a *group goal*—a single product (a set of answers, a project, a report, a piece or collection of creative writing, etc.) or achieving as high a *group average* as possible on a test—and then reward the entire group on the basis of the quality or quantity of its product according to a set standard of success. (p. 210)

Our strategies conform with this broad definition rather than falling under a specific model. The theme of this definition is carried down the line of educational evolution (from theorist proposal to field modification) by continually emerging interpretations of cooperative learning. For example, Anne Wheelock (1992) states:

> The most commonly mentioned teaching change in untracking schools is the shift from traditional teacher-centered instruction to cooperative learning. What does such a change entail? Dr. Robert Slavin of Johns Hopkins describes some of the characteristics of cooperative-learning classrooms. Heterogeneous grouping, including special education students, is the norm. Teachers and students share leadership appropriately. Activities emphasize task accomplishment and maintenance of skills. Students share responsibility for one another's learning, with the most effective learning evolving from positive interdependence among students. Teachers observe and intervene, teaching social skills directly. Students are held individually accountable for performance. Groups reflect on their effectiveness. (p. 200)

As we stated earlier, we are not presenting a new model of cooperative learning. What we are presenting, in terms of classroom work, are strategies that demand cooperative work and agree with broad and professionally constructed definitions of cooperative learning.

Throughout our activities we present social studies learning as a shared and cooperative venture. Our strategies outline opportunities for students to listen to the ideas of others and to redefine their own ideas according to the dialogue.

A NOTE ABOUT RESTRUCTURING

In the course of this book we refer often to *restructuring,* a term that may need some clarification for our purposes. Some schools of thought view restructuring as having a specific purpose such as altering the decision-making procedures in schools or creating new roles for teachers and administrators. Other more encompassing plans include a shift from tracked to mixed-ability classrooms.

We have seen the issue of heterogeneous classrooms impact our work and the way our school is organized. We also see a move from tracking to fit under the umbrella of restructuring that is presented within the literature. For example, Michael Fullan (1991) uses restructuring to mean a change in the structure of a "school as a workplace" (p. 87). In this view one of the conditions for restructuring includes changes in the "organizational arrangements" (1991, p. 88). Glickman (1991), in an essay addressing the tasks of restructuring, begins with the issue of "tracking" (1991, p. 5). David (1991) states that "restructuring requires all parts of the educational system to change, from students and teachers up through the myriad bureaucratic layers to the nation's capital" (p. 11). In each of these examples, restructuring offers a rubric that encompasses a number of components of change within the organization of a school. Teachers and students are linked to that organization because it structures their relationships on a daily basis. Research such as that of Nowicki (1992, 1993) suggests that shifting the way a school is organized from rigid tracks to mixed-ability classrooms alters faculty lives in many ways. Clearly, heterogeneous grouping is associated with organizational change and altering the way relationships exist in the structure of a school. This finding is consistent with John Goodlad's suggestion that "tracking is an organizational arrangement" (1984, p. 150) and reminds us that "tracking is listed in the educational literature under school organization" (Goodlad, 1984, p. 151). Clearly, a shift away from tracking alters the way roles are arranged in a school, including those of both students and teachers. Oakes tells us that the tracked school "organizes instruction" (1985, p. 6). The tracking issue is clearly tied in with the way schools are organized. As Nowicki states, "tracking is an organizational arrangement for everyone who is part of a school. It is a way to structure lives" (1992, p. 78). Moves toward heterogeneous grouping do fall within the general rubric of restructuring.

ALTERNATIVE REALITIES IN THE NONTRACKED CLASSROOM

The strategies that this book presents also reflect the social-educational world of the heterogeneous classroom. Although the strategies apply to any social studies classroom, all have been used in nontracked settings.

Social studies offers the history of social life and a means for understanding that life in the present. Human experience is a reflection of diversity. No two of us are completely alike in our thoughts and how we view the world around us. We interpret what we see differently as we are distinctive in the way we think. What we consider to be socially problematic often differs, as do the solutions we construct for those problems.

Yet we often organize our classrooms according to a master plan that limits interaction and dialogue. Tracking is one such organizational tool that groups students with like social behaviors. However, such tracking creates an artificial social situation in the classroom that does not reflect the ideals of diversity and heterogeneity we celebrate as goals in an open and democratic society such as the United States.

Conversely, the cooperative and nontracked social studies class does replicate society. In an election we do not base a person's right to vote on intellectual ability. Nor do we allow people to attend the town meeting, the bastion of participatory democracy, only if they are in a top group. The nontracked classroom offers a blending of perspectives from many individuals.

A growing body of literature supports heterogeneous grouping in classrooms. This work includes the national perspectives of Goodlad (1984), Oakes (1985, 1986), Oakes and Lipton (1990, 1992), George (1987), and Glazer (1990). Other advocates of detracking include Slavin (1987, 1988, 1990), Evans (1991), and Veves (1989). As a high school teacher and researcher, Nowicki has reported how teachers (Nowicki, 1990, 1991a, 1992) and students (Nowicki, 1991b, 1993) have responded to heterogeneous grouping in a public junior or senior high school. The movement away from tracked schools is grounded in evidence of successful efforts at educational restructuring. It offers both educators and students opportunities for redefining the nature of learning and the content of a social studies curriculum.

Some will argue that not all students can hold their own in the nontracked social studies classroom. Others speak about students being held back. Our experience tells us that students are held back socially and intellectually in tracked classrooms.

Students must be involved in their learning. They must create their own meaning from what they encounter in the social studies classroom. The diversity of the nontracked classroom offers a greater sharing of perspectives than the dialogue of the traditional tracked classroom. Likewise, the need to address the wide variety of learning styles in a heterogeneous classroom promotes the need to develop curriculum with a wide focus. When this occurs, the teacher begins to see the lessons of social studies coming alive. In giving up the traditional sense of control, teachers actually gain a greater and more meaningful form of guidance. They are directing and encouraging students to acquire knowledge, rather than controlling a class.

CHAPTER 2

A Model for Understanding the Components of a Lesson

Teachers often speak about the content of what they teach when explaining the importance of a particular lesson or the reasons to include a certain topic in the curriculum. In many ways the content, the nuts and bolts of subject matter, becomes the driving force shaping the organization of a class. Content frames the titles of individual courses and drives the structure of departmental and schoolwide courses of study. Content is the focus of textbooks, workbooks, and supplemental materials and testing. We teachers are defined by what we teach. We are not simply teachers; we are American history, world geography, or world history teachers.

Although the idea of what we teach occupies an important position, it often supersedes the idea of what students are learning in our classrooms. The two are completely interrelated, yet a lack of understanding remains as to exactly what happens as we teach our lessons. Consequently we feel a need to evaluate what we teach in terms of coverage and of time-based objectives. We all have heard the lines and may have used one or two ourselves in filling out our lesson plans. ("French Revolution this week up to page 454." "Reconstruction from pages 231 to 247." "The Pacific Northwest this week, Alaska and Hawaii next week.") We need to reflect further than "We'll cover Alaska this week." We need to examine a series of activities that enable us to understand what we are teaching and what our students are learning.

Educators in middle and senior high school classrooms need to focus on the linkages that exist between what they see as their message to students and the methodology used to transmit the message. These linkages require a closer examination of the foundation on which to build all lessons.

A THREE-WAY LOOK AT THE ELEMENTS OF A LESSON

Each lesson taught in a middle or senior high school social studies classroom can be broken down into at least three component areas. These areas are *factual knowledge, conceptual knowledge*, and *skill-based knowledge*. Each of these is equally important when one considers the whole of a lesson. Each represents a different problem for the teacher to consider in preparing and delivering a lesson. In addition to the three areas of knowledge, attention must also be given to other factors that concern far more than subject matter. Consequently, for teachers to activate and motivate learners, methods of instruction must also focus on integrating students into a participatory role with the curriculum.

Finding strategies that identify and use the three elements of a lesson is the first step to the goal of mastery. This is not necessarily a mastery that is global or over an entire discipline, nor one that claims complete understanding about a one hundred or one thousand year span of recorded history. Rather, it is an in-depth understanding of specific events in the human experience that can transcend the distance from a solitary event to a more holistic and critical perception about the social world in which we live.

Facts

If an area of learning in social studies has received an exaggerated importance, it is factual knowledge. Building a solid base of factual material should be one of the primary objectives for a social studies teacher. However, it should not be the only objective. For too many years a large number of social studies teachers relied on the rote memorization of facts. Some of the facts were and still are essential; others were superfluous accessories to curriculums that were limited in focus to two or three strategies of teaching and learning. Very often classes relied on lecture, note taking, reading, and answering the questions at the end of the chapter, followed by a multiple-choice or true-and-false test at the end of the week. Students were motivated by the threat of a bad grade or simply by the desire to show they could pass the course. Although a few actually thrived on this format because it fit the strengths of their personal learning styles, far more were, unfortunately, turned off and out of social studies.

In these cases the facts taught were vague and distant, with little connection to the world of the student. In a sense, facts were expected to stand on their own, encompassed by their own reality, not interconnected with other elements in the learning process. If facts had little meaning for students, classrooms structured to a predominantly factual dialogue became the breeding ground for unmotivated students. Furthermore, this format alienated students from what they were taught because the facts had no meaning outside of their own existence. It is easy for many of us to remember being forced to learn facts that we briefly held for a test and then promptly forgot. Resultantly the idea of fact memorization is etched in our society's collective consciousness.

Part of our problem in dealing with a multitude of facts originated with the people who taught us and wrote the course outlines. Some teachers saw themselves as curators of the complete base of knowledge of the social studies. They tried in their classes at the junior high school or high school to replicate the world they once encountered in the college lecture hall.

There were other teachers who were required to use an assigned text and follow a particular guide. They expected their students to take standardized tests that were prepared, in part, by the people who designed the curriculum guides and wrote the textbooks the teachers used. The focus again was on factual knowledge.

Administrators also contributed to the domination of facts over other elements in the learning process by being so obsessed with control and order in classrooms that teachers had no choice but to follow the lecture, note taking, questions at the end of the chapter, and quiz model. That routine did contribute to quiet, rigidly ordered classrooms. The teachers who ran those classrooms received few complaints. All the while, many students were continually removed from integrating, on a personal level of learning, what the social studies had to offer.

We are not advocating the elimination of students learning facts in the social studies classroom, however. They should. There are certain facts about the shaping of our collective experience that we all should know if we wish to be participants in building a creative future. We share a collective past as a civilization, a society, and as human beings. As such, terms and words exist whose recognition should provoke meaning for us. Everyone should know, recognize, and understand as important certain events, dates, and people because of their impact on the development of culture and civilization. To ignore facts is to abdicate our responsibility as social studies teachers. One need only consider certain revisionist claims that the Holocaust never happened to be reminded of our need to remember that certain facts should be taught, guarded, and protected by the social studies curriculum.

Although we have offered some criticism about the overreliance on factual learning in directing social studies curricula, we clearly do not wish to do away with it completely, as others have suggested. We believe such a move destroys a part of the scope social studies has to offer. We are advocating that social studies teachers recognize and use *factual-based learning* only when it is integrated with *concepts* and *skills* to complete a learning triangle for every lesson.

Concepts

Concepts have always held a place in social studies education. Our lessons incorporated them through the addition of an obligatory essay question on every test. We seem to have forgotten, however, that our own concepts underlie how we create meanings and understandings. Concepts are personal constructions based on acquiring and integrating the best evidence possible into a cohesive and coherent framework of ideas. Concepts deserve more than the tired old essay at the end of the factual test. They are the intellectual constructions that we use to make sense of ourselves and the world around us. Concepts are extremely important in any educational agenda.

To be sure, the word *concept* is difficult to define. Many educators have exclusively focused on defining the term. There are numerous definitions, many quite similar, that apply to our use of the term. Consequently we believe that we should help the reader come to a better understanding of how we use the term *concept*.

We view concepts as integral to the learning process. They represent a third of the triad shared with *skills* and *facts* as components of social studies lessons. To explain a concept, we need to examine the ideas and definitions presented in the past that underlie our view. These ideas offer a substantial insight into the way we shape our construct. For example, Marlin Tanck suggested that

> Concepts are generalized bodies of attributes associated with the symbol for a class of things, events, or ideas. (1969, p. 101, as cited by Chapin & Gross, 1973, p. 192)

Paul Brandwein suggests:

> A concept is a mental construct, isolating from experience the common attributes that identify objects and events. (1971, p. 32)

The idea of a constructivist approach, which runs through the strategies we present, supports our use of *concepts,* as each lesson outline indicates. The act of creating their own understandings and knowledge provides students with a level of ownership; they become vested in the process of construction. The constructivist approach to understanding the term *concept* is further suggested by the defining criteria proposed by Verna Fancett:

> A concept is an individual's own way of making meanings of things he has experienced. . . a mental image which assists a person in classifying his experiences, and which continually changes as his experiences accumulate. (1971, p. 14)

Our use of the term *concept* is grounded in the idea of lessons that enable students to recreate information into their vision and on their terms. In this view, learning becomes the students' responsibility. Teachers become guides. Barry Beyer provides a further definition and clarification of *concept:*

> A concept is a mental image of something. The "something" may be anything—a concrete object, a type of behavior, an abstract idea. This image has two basic dimensions—the individual components of the concept as well as the relationships of these components to each other and to the whole. (1971, p. 8)

Our use of the term meets the criteria set down in earlier definitions of *concepts* in the social studies. We realize there is not a perfect definition that will satisfy all demands. Yet, in terms of this work, our working definition of a *concept* includes the following elements:

- Concepts are ideas in a basic sense.

- The ideas that frame a concept include the interconnections of many diverse perspectives. We find this particularly true in the diversity represented within a mixed-ability classroom.

- Concepts are complex in that they require the support of other types of learning such as skills and factual information.

- Concepts not only represent singular ideas in the social studies but also complex interconnections that provide understanding accessible only by taking into account many separate ideas.

- Concepts are continuous recreations in which students and teachers redefine and create the possibilities of learning.

- Understanding a concept provides students with the *larger picture* of what they are doing in class as it is *tied* to their world. Concepts are grounded ultimately in the experience of living and the experience of learning.

Our use of *concepts* within this book focuses on what can be created and learned by the individual student. It is tied to the skills and facts that constitute every strategy we present.

Facts and concepts are not mutually exclusive; in fact, they rely on one another. Every lesson taught in the social studies deals with both. Facts provide the bones on which a concept takes shape. Concepts provide a large picture in which facts suddenly take on meaning. As analysis and interpretation occurs to create new conceptual frameworks, a higher level of knowledge develops. For students, the meanings that a true conceptual understanding bring are very personal. But more importantly, conceptual understanding serves as the stepping stone to higher-level understanding. Concepts are not only important intellectual constructions and guides for interpreting the world around us; they are also the cognitive building blocks we use as we continue to inquire about our world and our part in it.

Too often concepts have not been included in the educational milieu nor given their due. Conceptual understandings are sometimes perceived as being difficult to evaluate by classroom teachers. Those trying to address an audience larger than the classroom may tend to view concepts as controlled in the subjective world and therefore not open to effective and objective evaluation. However, to negate the importance of concepts is to unplug the metaphoric lightbulb that goes on in our heads when we have made a discovery that makes our lives better in some way. For those discoveries, some of which go far beyond our own limited world, all carry the power of breakthrough recognition about who we are and what an event means.

As educators we must strive to achieve educational excellence among our students and to build a society that is socially and historically literate. To this end we must promote and nurture those conceptual understandings made by our students. We need to escape from the overreliance on evaluating what students learn on a purely factual basis. We believe it is the *conceptual* understanding that highlights the connections between the *facts* and the *skills* to frame what we teach.

Once the connections are made, we can increase students' intellectual readiness and begin to focus them on the truly important conceptual discoveries. At that point and on their terms, we come to understand all students as individuals and as members of a similar cohort.

Skills

Our focus on what students as a class and as individual learners gain through factual and conceptual learning brings our discussion back to the beginning and forward to the conclusion of what classroom education should be. To understand factual material and create conceptual understandings, students must be competent at using the skills involved in learning.

We expect students to develop thinking and learning skills. Some of these skills are subject specific. Others are linked to a more general social studies perspective. Still others are global and include all levels and areas of learning. Each area of skills is linked, either directly or indirectly, to application in later life and to what we encounter as *fact* and develop as *concept*. The trouble is that we attempt to evaluate intellectual mastery of facts or concepts based on what a student can or cannot do. In schools we look toward what is often termed "basic skills." These are certainly essential to any learning that takes place in our schools. But skills, outside of remedial skills at the junior or senior high school level, do not gain the attention that is given the other products of learning such as facts or concepts. Evaluation is part of the problem. Skills that enhance learning at higher levels are difficult to evaluate. Often skill evaluation is on the production line model. What the students produce reflects both factual knowledge and skill. If they do not demonstrate the factual knowledge, they receive a poor grade. However, educators should be concerned that students are not sufficiently taught the higher-level skills (Bloom, 1956) that will enfranchise them in their learning. We believe that skills allow students to integrate the content matter of a course of studies into their own knowledge base.

Bloom and others (1956) clearly identified this progression of learning along a taxonomy that established six stages of student learning (Figure 2.1). As students become fluent in each step, they spiral upward, at each level becoming more proficient and able to think on a higher level. The taxonomy identifies the first level of learning as *knowledge in the sense of recognition and recall* (p. 62). The information gained from this stage allows students to progress to *comprehension* (p. 89), where they work through translation, interpretation, and extrapolation of the knowledge they had acquired. This unlocks the next door to *application* (p. 120), as students apply the information to problem-solving areas and consider solutions. Once proficient at this step, students continue the upward spiral to the level of *analysis* (p. 144) as they classify and examine relationships of what they are developing. This skill leads the learners to the two highest levels of thinking and learning: *synthesis* (p. 162) and *evaluation* (p. 185). At the *synthesis* level the student digests the knowledge of the previous four stages and uses that information to create a product showing comprehension in a different mode. For example, students could extend a

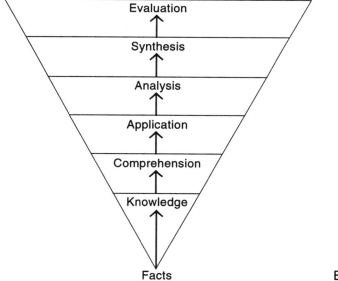

FIGURE 2.1
Bloom's Taxonomy

short story for two pages after examining it through the first four areas of knowledge acquisition. Finally in the taxonomy the student is able to make judgments and evaluate the worth of something: what is good or bad, moral or immoral, and important or not important (Figure 2.2).

We offer a model that also makes use of a spiraling progression of acquiring information as a means of reaching a greater understanding of how we gain knowledge. In an analysis of every lesson taught one should expect to find identifiable *factual knowledge, conceptual knowledge*, and *skill-based knowledge*. Each should reflect the diversity of

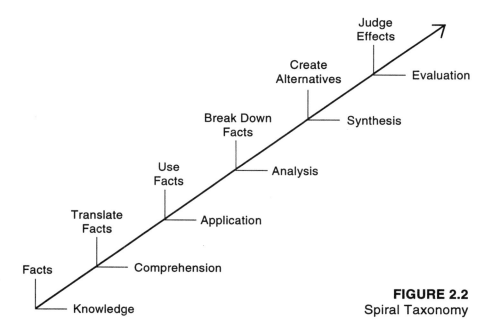

FIGURE 2.2
Spiral Taxonomy

learners that compose a classroom and the needs of each of those learners. To rule out one student from success in participating in a social studies class because that student lacks the ability to memorize or to read critically ignores other skills essential to the learning process. For example, a student who is a lower-level reader could become the person to organize and manage a class research project. Because a student reads at a level below peers in no way diminishes the student's ability to organize and manage.

Thus *skills* are an integral component of any social studies lesson. They are linked to *factual learning* and to *developing conceptual understandings*. However, there are other considerations that enter into and infringe on the satisfactory development of teaching strategies using these three components to a lesson. These concerns must be addressed in developing a model for designing any strategies for the social studies classroom.

MATCHING THE STRATEGIES WITH THE CURRICULUM

The three component elements we have highlighted reflect what we teach in our courses. These strategies encourage our access of each element in a lesson rather than overloading our attention on one of the three. However, there are two inhibitors restricting these strategies. The first is the curriculum itself. There needs to be a fit in meshing strategies to the curriculum to be taught. The fit need not be perfect but should be flexible enough to allow the individual classroom teacher the power to make sound educational judgments reflecting teacher and student needs. We have too often felt the pain of having to fit our strategies to the demands of the curriculum rather than to the needs of our students. That is why the strategies contained in the next four chapters are not meant to be followed in a rigid fashion. If they work exactly as we have outlined, that is wonderful. If they need to be modified to meet the needs of a particular classroom and diverse group of learners, that is fine also. If they need to be constantly loaded toward one side of the three elements involved in a lesson to adhere to an inflexible curriculum, then modification becomes unacceptable in our view. The curriculum should not have sole ownership of teaching strategies. Teachers must have more power to influence curriculum and methodology.

THE ISSUE OF TIME

A second inhibitor of creating and fully using new and different teaching strategies is the issue of time. There are only so many days a teacher can be teaching in a classroom. Schoolwide events cut into that time. Curriculum-driven classes are always propelled by the sheer force of the amount of material to be covered. History teachers in those instances are like train engineers, trying to be at a certain place at a certain time as their classroom train highballs its way across the railroad of time. We have been in this situation. Some of our conversations have taken on some strange tones when the two of us have been teaching a survey course about World History. Usually we find two minutes in passing from one class to another, take out our calendars, and begin talking in hushed tones. Anyone passing and caring enough to listen would hear talk such as, "You'll be in Babylon on the 14th, Joe? Then I'll be in Athens by the 5th." And, "OK, Kerry, in that case I'll have us in Rome by the 8th and watching the Republic fall by the 10th." Imagine what the uninitiated listener would think.

Part of our need "to be places at near enough the same time" is self-inflicted. We happen to believe that history is a series of sequential events in which one event leads to another. To understand how and why one event happens, you need to know the past. We also believe there are themes that run through all of history as each successive people asks the same questions as did the people before, searching for answers that they can agree on rather than the existing ones that do not seem to fit.

Yet there are special circumstances individual teachers face that we think need more attention. We are teachers who are not bound by a state- or county-mandated curriculum that requires us to "be at a certain place by a certain time." We set our own expectations concerning coverage, although we do have a district curriculum we follow.

We have a degree of freedom many social studies teachers do not have, but we share common concerns. We always feel we are running out of time. Our work in World History is always fraught with not addressing recent historical fact. The same concern is true in any of the other ten courses we collectively teach. Yet issues of current global, societal, and interpersonal life run through our strategies. Our efforts are geared to connecting students living in the present with the experience of the past. We believe this focus can be incorporated into any mixed-ability social studies classroom regardless of mandated curriculum. Teachers may take one, ten, or twenty of our strategies and adapt them for their classrooms and fit them into their curriculums.

What we present is not meant to supplant the curriculum a teacher follows. Our work is to aid teachers in designing their curriculum, activities, and strategies. We present strategies to supplement the work of teachers and make learning more involving and constructivist for students. We encourage teachers to try our strategies in their classrooms in ways they believe can best serve their students.

Implementing these strategies within a classroom comes down to what individual teachers wish to do with their students. It also assumes a level of control we believe teachers should have as professionals structuring the learning of their students. Teachers need to budget time. Teachers, working effectively as guides, need to set the course. To revert to worries about issues of coverage and let those worries inhibit the creation of learning experiences open to all learners is to regress into a fact-driven curriculum.

In summary, time is an issue that social studies teachers need to balance. Although for each strategy we recommend a time frame, these are merely adaptable suggestions. Furthermore, based on time constraints, the teacher may decide whether to use the activity to structure a direct content area or as a supplemental resource. However, we hope our suggestions will assist teachers in having some control over the ever present issue of time.

STUDENT-DIRECTED–TEACHER-GUIDED LEARNING AS A MEANS OF INQUIRY

If classroom teachers are to have more control over the curricula they teach, their students also need to have a similar sense of ownership. A cooperative teaching and learning strategy dictates a collegial relationship between teachers and students. The strategies we present are based on cooperative and mutually inclusive relationships in which teachers and students have worked in an atmosphere of mutual respect. This contrasts with the experiences we have had working in classrooms and in schools that reflected the sense of tension when ownership and control are one-sided propositions. Too often, as we pointed out earlier, classrooms relying on one style of teaching and overplaying the importance of one component of lessons foster division by alienating students from their learning and from their teachers. Similarly, strictly limiting teachers' ability to design their own curriculum and constraining the strategies that can be used in actual teaching alienates teachers from their craft and from their students.

Cooperative strategies demand that we reconfigure many of the relationships that persist in schooling. We must continue perfecting the model by which students direct their learning and teachers become the guides for learning experiences. Such a model reflects the teaching-learning relationship in the truest sense. It is not cluttered with emotional issues created by the tug of power often found in a completely teacher-directed classroom.

Enfranchising students as directors of their learning brings life into schooling and produces the type of learner we believe is essential to our society. For example, the self-directed student has the courage to experiment and the security to work on his or her own without needing constant prodding and direction. The middle, junior high, or senior high school teacher who redefines the professional role to that of guide is also empowered in many ways. The teacher sets the overall agenda. The teacher establishes the big picture that considers both learning objectives relative to the needs and ages of students and the content of the class. The teacher recognizes the position of the course in the scope and sequence of the larger school and district curriculum. The teacher provides the opportunities for experimentation and exploration that empower students to become directors of specific learning situations.

We have found that when our roles begin to take on the look of guide and students are enabled to take greater control of their roles as learners, discipline loses primacy as an issue. We also have found that when our classrooms do not demand that we become the sole source for all learning and knowledge, our preparation is different, more creative, more stimulating, and more fun. Although we do not always replicate the ideal in all of our classrooms, newer strategies and a greater involvement with mutual trust allow for error without destruction. Some days everything works to perfection; on other days, it bombs. As any teacher knows, an enormous number of variables can influence a classroom's climate. For example, in a class of twenty-five eighth graders, a multitude of imponderables exists that can have both positive and negative impacts on the group. The noneducational demands faced by teachers add to the complexity of the situation. Consequently teachers need help in acquiring strategies and activities to do the job in a professional and effective manner. Cooperative classrooms answer many of these concerns.

THE OWNERSHIP OF IDEAS

We have stressed the importance of creating a sense of ownership over what occurs in the classroom for both teachers and students. We believe that ownership, either individually or cooperatively, represents student-created meanings, either singly or in groups, within the classroom. We present examples taken from our classrooms in which students were directors of their own learning and teachers the guides. Their ideas, generated through the use of the strategies, were their own. This scenario is far different from one in which the teacher gives and the students take, reject, or ignore. The words, insights, and understandings of another are meaningless unless examined by an individual and woven into his or her personal knowledge base. By developing and using the processes that create those understandings, we can give importance to the development of ideas.

PERSONAL THEORY BUILDING AND RESEARCH: BRINGING IDEAS TO LIFE

We also must look at the way we design the process of inquiry in our classrooms. Inquiry into a topic demands that one possess the skills to conduct research that leads to the design of intellectual interpretations and constructions. It is research that allows us to create the interpretations to help us navigate through life. These interpretations form the basis for our theories.

Education should operate in the same way. Students conducting inquiry and research into topics of interest begin first to develop personal knowledge. From that knowledge base, they create a theoretical framework. From this framework they move to the highest level of knowledge acquisition: theory building.

We need to encourage our students to develop and build theories based on the evidence they discover. In developing new strategies that integrate learning for all students, we recognize that students and teachers are both important theory builders. We need further to develop theory builders because by encouraging their expertise and working together in directed and guided cooperative learning relationships, students and teachers foster the strategy for future use.

In developing theory building, students gain appreciation for evaluating both the method of inquiry and the conclusions from that inquiry. This individual and self-reflective critique is part of the process of presentation and discussion. It is part of the dialogue of the classroom. It is based on the knowledge that students can and will produce evidence to defend their theories. As a result it begins to replicate for them the daily encounters of forming ideas and taking positions in their own lives.

In the process of forming, researching, and presenting the theories, the three component parts of a lesson indispensably culminate and merge. For example, for students to develop and present a theory, they need evidence based on a body of knowledge (*factual material*). Students need to acquire knowledge through a disciplined inquiry (reflecting our emphasis on *research skills*). They then need to merge the findings of their collected evidence and interpretations to create ideas (*conceptual understandings*).

But the process is still not complete. In the final stage a synthesis of the three elements drives the lessons. The presentation of developed conclusions (*theories*) to a public audience of peers and others proves the effectiveness of the process. Consequently the results of the activity and theory building are shared with the rest of a class as well as the teacher. But more importantly this public presentation of final conclusions is not simply a product but a continuation of the process of learning. It serves as the basis to begin inquiry anew in a manner that constantly takes from the base of the past and applies that base to the information generated by the future.

Again the role for the teacher in such a model is participant guide. The teacher encourages the exploration that leads to information gathering. The teacher helps frame the critique of research strategy and depth. The teacher fosters the experimentation with ideas that lead to conceptual understandings as the students seek the internal direction that kindles creativity and experimentation.

TEACHERS AND STUDENTS AS SELF-EVALUATORS

Effective evaluation must occur to nurture theory building that leads to the presentation of a final product blending a knowledge of *fact*, *skill*, and *concept*. In the classroom that recognizes student ownership of knowledge, students also must share ownership of evaluation and assessment. But evaluation is a very sticky issue in any educational endeavor. Students sharing their work with peers in a public forum are engaging in a very powerful example of peer evaluation. Reflective evaluations focus students on the worth and meaning of their own creations. In every part of the learning experience the teacher is also an evaluator. Teachers, the knowledgeable guides, are integral to the issue of evaluation but are not the sole source of critique. Our aim is to integrate and not to separate. This holds true for grading. The grade must be the result of shared input and decision making, assessing all three component parts, *facts, skills*, and *concepts*. Evaluation must be a learning tool that influences students' experiences. In this way it is not a means of ranking students but a dialogue in which student accomplishment is refined and improved. We believe our strategies offer exactly those types of opportunities.

CHAPTER 3

The Interview

FOUR TYPES OF TEACHING STRATEGIES

Four specific types of interview strategies fall within the larger format of teaching strategies that we have included under the general heading of "The Interview." Each strategy requires some level of student-to-student or student-to-other interviewing. These strategies, which are multifaceted and student centered, use the information gained in the interviewing process to generate a final product. In each case the students are the reporters, the investigators, and the producers of their work. These strategies encourage ownership of work by particular students as well as by groups of students working cooperatively toward a common goal. Often these classroom strategies are not only intellectually rewarding but are fun to complete.

The Interview

As social beings who need communication with others to succeed, we continually engage in conversations. Our very being demands that we speak with others to exchange our ideas, to share our insights, to express our doubts, and to deliver our challenges. Following this pattern of behavior and discourse, interviews are at the heart of what it means to be human. Today students are constantly being exposed to the personal nature of interviews in the mass media. From *CNN* to *Entertainment Tonight* to radio and television talk shows, interviews are a major source of current knowledge as well as entertainment. Consequently an interview is an activity for which students already have a frame of reference to create their own systems for acquiring information and gaining knowledge. Yet we often ignore the importance of conversation as an educational tool.

As teachers we must take advantage of the skills that students already possess and work with them to hone and to generalize these skills to the arena of academic achievement. Students can then begin to operate on a comfort level based on something students love to do: talk. It then becomes our job as teachers to shift the students' question from "What did you do last night?" asked of the girl next to them to "What did you do last night?" to the Roman gladiator. Once students assume the first person persona that an interview demands, they begin to personalize the information they are acquiring. Therefore, as they begin to share the information it becomes more powerful than a standard report. A report merely imparts information; an interview explains and shares knowledge.

When teachers in the social studies classroom use the interview as a teaching strategy, students develop an appreciation for questioning skills and listening skills. Interviews can be focused and follow an explicit guide or be more open ended and conversational and yet continue to follow an established topic. The student interviewer must gain information about the social studies topic from another person through a series of clearly articulated questions. Within these roles students can be subjects as well as questioners in role play situations in the documentary and the news report activities. Additionally, the interview lends itself to embracing resource persons outside of the classroom and through their words bringing them into the school.

The people with whom we share society are resources to every social studies classroom at the junior or senior high school. Interviews offer the opportunity to access the information those resources hold. Whether the topic of an interview concerns a current issue, such as a parent's view of mandatory education, or a World War II veteran's recollections, the interview is an effective means for adding to the flavor of a classroom.

Interviewing also demands that students be prepared for this process of inquiry by effectively researching the topic in question. Similarly, students must also develop their analytical skills as they sift through the words of others for insights and patterns. The development of students' listening skills is essential to this process. Students must also cultivate the skills for data recording. For longer, more in-depth interviews, students may need to use audiotape, requiring them to learn to compile written transcriptions from the tape as a means for reviewing data. For interviews taking a shorter span of time, students would be required to extend their note taking and hand transcription skills. In both cases, the recorded and transcribed data or summaries of the data serve as the basis for analysis.

Interviews can be used to provide a supplement to the classroom or the actual content for a class. For example, in Joe's American Studies class focusing on the Great Depression of the 1930s, interviews were conducted with community members who had lived through the depression. These interviews formed a supplementary resource. Later, in a subsequent class, the two hundred typed and bound pages of interview transcriptions from the members of the American Studies class became the basis for the course content and relegated the standard text to reference status. As with other strategies, the length and scope of interviews as well as the time frame when interviews are conducted and transcribed are all established by both teacher and students.

The Documentary

One group of strategies centers around the *documentary*. This approach to discovering information through individual and group research also includes presenting the product to others. The documentary, in a simple sense, is a means to tell a story about an event, a place, a period of time, a particular person, or a group of people. Its focus is singular in that the report is based on an in-depth study of a specific topic rather than a cursory treatment of a variety of topics. It could be as specific as a look at Leonardo DaVinci or as broad as "The Artistic Advancements of the Renaissance."

The documentary is different from the traditional research report. The documentary is a collaborative strategy involving the work of a group or a team of students rather than of a single individual. Students must work together because of the diversity of roles and responsibilities involved in documentary production. Student roles include being the subjects of the documentary and the researchers, artists, and videographers. The documentary, like the traditional research report, requires a final product for presentation. Unlike the research report, the product of this strategy is not a typed report but a presentation that is either audiotaped or videotaped.

A documentary project can serve as the central activity for a section of course material or it can be used as a continuing supplement to work in progress. It combines factual information with a presentation of conceptual understandings. This strategy introduces students to skills such as researching a topic, building a bibliography, framing questions to document certain information, asking questions, designing a multimedia presentation, and using technology for presenting knowledge in entertaining and informative ways. This strategy also can be used to reinforce these skills.

The News Report

The news report is also a group-directed presentation that can use a multimedia approach. Similar to the documentary, the news report involves the reporting of an event or events through audiotape, videotape, still photography, or print. Unlike the documentary, the news report presents events as taking place in an up-to-date fashion. The final result is a product that is publicly presented as a work reflecting contemporary times. The news report offers students the ability to be as creative as they wish in designing the report. The number of actual "reports" contained in the final product is again at the discretion of the teacher and the group. However, each correspondent's report might feature different angles and interesting side bars to the main topic. For example, a news report on the assassination of the Archduke Ferdinand might also feature interviews with those innocent victims injured in the bombing or the policeman who arrived first on the scene as well as reports on and interviews with the principals directly involved or affected.

The news report strategy is flexible enough to be used as a primary activity, a supplement to other class work, or an end of the term project. It can be used for varying lengths of time, from two days to two weeks.

Some of the benefits of this strategy are that it involves factual learning, conceptual understandings, and skill mastery. Furthermore, it is grounded in the interpersonal dialogue that frames most current news reports that students see every night on television, and it uses that interpersonal dialogue in a final product. It additionally reinforces the skills that contribute to effective research, note taking, and synthesizing that information into an entertaining and creative presentation of knowledge.

Some of our experiences with news reports are memorable. For example, Joe has watched ninth graders take their reporting very seriously, to the point of becoming combative. The simple news report turned into an additional editorial comment. This in turn set the stage for others to arrange the news in terms that were agreeable to political perspectives. In many ways, especially in the election years of 1988 and 1992, students tended to take an extra interest in what was taking place in the classroom because many of the themes were similar.

In other instances, news reports have been a benefit to the school community. They became a means of taking the information from a class and presenting it to the rest of the school community. To be sure, sometimes the camera does not record or the tape recorder malfunctions. We have always found a way as teachers and students to rise above what can go wrong.

The Thought Question

As a shorter variation of the interview, the thought question offers the opportunity for directly integrating the worlds without and within the classroom. The thought question is designed to be used primarily as a supplement to work in the classroom. It is a simple strategy yet a powerful tool in bridging the gap that sometimes occurs between the world of the classroom and the world beyond.

Simply put, a thought question is generated from the material covered in a specific unit or lesson. It usually reflects what is perceived as a problematic issue, one that is a constant source of negotiation for everyone in society. The issue addressed is one that has been dealt with in the past, is still being dealt with today, and will probably be dealt with in the future.

The thought question generally evolves when a student is asked, or asks, a question in class that relates to a topic of study. For example, an issue in World History could be, Was the dropping of the atomic bomb at Hiroshima and Nagasaki necessary? The student then asks this question of others, usually adults, outside the classroom or the school. The student records the adult's answer and reports to the rest of the class on the following day. Lengthwise, thought questions seek answers that are restricted to a page.

The thought questions that we offer in this chapter have initiated powerful dialogue between students in the classroom and adults outside. For both interviewer and the interview subject, the conceptual learning that occurs for both parties is insightful and meaningful and provides an added sense of life and relevancy to the current social studies topic and classroom.

Sample Interview Strategies

Course:	World History
Length of Activity:	One day
Grade Level:	9
Unit:	World War I
Topic:	The Rise of Communism in Europe
Title:	A Press Conference with Friedreich Engels and Karl Marx
Description of Activity:	**(Circle one)** **Documentary News Report (Interview) Thought Question**
Overview:	It is very important for students to understand the ideas and the beliefs that create political and economic systems. Communism was a natural outgrowth of political and economic pressures in Europe as a result of the industrial revolution and the changes that this brought about in the daily life. However, the ideas of Marx, Engels, and Lenin framed communism. To understand these ideas, have a press conference and ask the two gentlemen to explain their beliefs.
Number of Students:	20
List of Roles:	Karl Marx, Friedreich Engels, V. I. Lenin, and a moderator. Each remaining student will function as a member of the press corps with a prepared series of questions (If space is available, two press conferences can be scheduled, thereby involving two more students in the key roles of **Marx** and **Engels**).
Concepts:	1. Effect of economics on political systems 2. Social democracy 3. Socialism 4. Communism 5. Capitalism
Factual Information:	Karl Marx, totalitarian state, industrial revolution, bourgeoisie, *Communist Manifesto,* Friedreich Engels, proletariat, V. I. Lenin.
Skills:	1. Asking leading and interpretive questions 2. Inferential skills 3. Critical thinking 4. Personal theory building

Timetable of Activities:

TIME FRAME (BY WEEK/BY DAY)

(Day 1)   Assign roles

(Day 2)   Presentation of the press conference

Evaluation:

1. Evaluate the presentation, with emphasis on the thoroughness of research, the accuracy of questions and answers, and the effort involved in preparing questions and answers.

2. Students will write a short response to press conference. They will stress (a) the major ideas of each figure; (b) what they believe the key points are from their point of view; (c) what conditions in Europe in this period contributed to the rise of communism.

Corollaries to Murphy's Law:

Although the time limits given are for two days, that is not necessarily a total amount of two days' time. The roles can be assigned on a Monday with the presentation scheduled for two or three days later, depending on how much time is needed for the students to prepare their roles. However, we have found this type of activity is best kept on a tight schedule. Too much time leads to procrastination.

Course: Civics

Length of Activity: Two days

Grade Level: 7–8

Unit: Government

Topic: Town/Municipal Government

Title: Knowing a Local Official

Description of Activity:

(Circle one)

Documentary   News Report   (Interview)   Thought Question

Overview: This activity is designed to complement a unit on local government. All students are required to interview a government official and report on the interview. Each student will follow an interview guide developed by the class. The interview guide should contain no more than ten questions. Students turn in written reports of the interviews, including their reactions to the interview.

Number of Students: 20–25

List of Roles: All students as interviewers

Concepts:
1. The many duties and responsibilities of government officials
2. The need to have effective government if society is to function

Factual Information: List of officials to be interviewed, their duties, how they are placed in office, their salary if any

Skills:
1. Interviewing and reporting
2. Learning how to use government

Timetable of Activities:

TIME FRAME (BY WEEK/BY DAY)

(Day 1)   Interviews are conducted over a period set up by the class. The interviews are reported as a one-day activity.

Evaluation: Student oral and written reports

Corollaries to
Murphy's Law: Teacher needs to make sure enough government officials in the area will agree to spend time with students. Enough lead time should be given to students to line up the interview subject. In small towns this can be a problem.

Course:	World History
Length of Activity:	One week
Grade Level:	9
Unit:	World War I
Topic:	Causes of War
Title:	The Assassination of the Archduke

Description of Activity:

(Circle one)

~~Documentary~~ News Report   Interview   Thought Question

Overview: The concept of historical chance is an important idea for students to understand. Do events just happen or do they need a "trigger" to set in motion the actions that bring about the larger and more influential event? This activity focuses the students on the situation in pre-war Europe as they examine the assassination and its effects on the tense European alliances.

Number of Students: 20

List of Roles: Gavrilo Princip, a Serbian Nationalist, Kaiser Wilhelm, an Austrian diplomat, the ruler of Austria-Hungry, the Serbian nationalist who threw the bomb, the Serbian nationalist who lost his nerve and did nothing, the Russian czar, British Prime Minister, President Wilson

Concepts:

1. The impact of historical chance

2. The rising influence of militarism, nationalism, and imperialism

3. The purpose and effect of national alliances

Factual Information: Triple Alliance, Triple Entente, The Black Hand, Archduke Francis Ferdinand, Austria-Hungary, the Balkans, Serbia, Slavic Nationalism, Ottoman Empire, Kaiser Wilhelm, the Austria-Hungarian Ultimatum, Serbs, Croats, Slovenes, Yugoslavia, June 28, 1914, July 28, 1914

Skills:

1. Further development of inferential thinking skills

2. Ability to locate Sarajevo on the map

3. Create a map showing the Triple Entente and the Triple Alliance

4. Library research skills

5. Assuming a first person persona to subjectivize historical data

**Timetable of
Activities:**

TIME FRAME (BY WEEK/BY DAY)

(Day 1)   Assign roles and partnerships

(Day 2)   Research and writing

(Day 3)   Research and writing

(Day 4)   Rehearse

(Day 5)   Presentation

Evaluation: Evaluation will be based on the effectiveness of the presentations; especially important are accuracy of research, supporting evidence of inferences, and thoroughness and seriousness of presentation.

**Corollaries to
Murphy's Law:** Students must realize that a certain amount of work must be completed outside of the class. As students are working on this the class work will continue on to other areas of the beginning of the war. However, the teacher needs to create provisions for absentee students.

Course:	World History
Length of Activity:	Five days
Grade Level:	9
Unit:	The Middle Ages
Topic:	The Manorial System
Title:	A Day on the Manor of Lord Chauncey
Description of Activity:	**(Circle one)**
	⟨Documentary⟩ News Report Interview Thought Question
Overview:	The manorial system was a powerful political/economic system that dominated Europe in the Middle Ages. It offered security, protection, and a self-sufficient way of life to a full spectrum of people. Students need to understand how the system functioned, both politically and economically, to have a foundation for understanding the Middle Ages and the subsequent growth of towns and cities.
Number of Students:	20
List of Roles:	Lord Chauncey, his wife, various serfs (cook, carpenter, blacksmith, field hand), a knight, his page, a freeman, the parish priest, Lady Chauncey's lady in waiting
Concepts:	Feudalism, the manorial system, foundations for growth of cities and towns
Factual Information:	Serfs, manor, self-sufficient, lie fallow, page, primogeniture, joust, squire, Code of Chivalry, vassal, fief, Vikings, tournament, lay investiture, medieval
Skills:	1. Library research
	2. Critical thinking skills
	3. Developing leading questions
	4. Historical diagramming
	5. Creating historical subjectivity by writing, speaking in a first person persona

Timetable of Activities:

TIME FRAME (BY WEEK/BY DAY)

(Day 1) Assign roles and partners for activity, research

(Day 2) Research—a few minutes in class—rest as homework

(Day 3) Research—homework

(Day 4) In class time—writing—rehearsing

(Day 5) Presentations

Evaluation: Evaluation of presentation will concentrate on accuracy of information, thoroughness of research, amount of effort, use of additional props and teaching tools, visuals

Corollaries to Murphy's Law: An issue to be wary of in this scenario is how to hold the final presentation. There are two ways of doing this. One is to have the students put the whole project together and then videotape it for presentation to the class. The other is to present the project and videotape the presentation. Both ways have benefits. Early in the year it is sometimes more effective to have the students spend the class time putting the project together and videotaping each segment. Then put all the segments together into the documentary. As the students become more proficient, more of the technical aspects can be left to them. Additionally they develop their own sense of flow and timing. The important thing for the teacher to remember is not to quit on an idea. The first time is rocky as everyone learns the process. Keep working on it and the process becomes very smooth and effective.

Course: World History

Length of Activity: Two weeks

Grade Level: 9

Unit: World War I

Topic: The Causes, the War, and the Aftermath

Title: A Documentary on World War I

Description of Activity:

(Circle one)

(Documentary) News Report   Interview   Thought Question

Overview: This is a continuous activity that occurs over the entire unit of World War I. Roles are assigned very early in the unit, and students are responsible for researching their roles and their scripts. They must work in conjunction with the news correspondents who will interview them to develop probing questions and thoughtful, insightful answers. The final product is then presented as a summarizer for the war before the test on World War I.

Number of Students: 20

List of Roles: Woodrow Wilson, Georges Clemanceau, Gavrilo Princip, General John Pershing, Lenin, Erich Maria Remarque, David Lloyd George, Vittorio Orlando, Kaiser Wilhelm, commanders of the French and the German forces at Verdun, a French soldier (victim of mustard gas who survived), a German soldier who fought throughout the war, an American doughboy, Adolf Hitler, a German citizen, a French citizen, two videographers

Concepts:
1. Militarism, imperialism, and nationalism as major causes of the war

2. A total, world war

3. Understanding cause and effect on global scale

4. Isolationism

Factual Information: Franz Ferdinand, 1914, Bismarck, Kaiser Wilhelm, Ottoman Empire, Triple Alliance, Triple Entente, Western Front, Eastern Front, Battles of Verdun, Marne, Allies, Central Powers, U-boat, Zimmermann note, Treaty of Brest Litovsk, Woodrow Wilson, Treaty of Versailles, war guilt, reparations, trench warfare, Lusitania, November 11, 1918, Austria-Hungary, Slavic Nationalism, The Black Hand, Gavrilo Princip, Bosnia Herzegovina

Skills:
1. Creating a time line

2. Creating and comparing maps of pre- and post-war Europe

3. Recognizing and differentiating cause and effect

4. Using critical thinking skills in putting together a "big picture"

5. Using historical subjectivity

Timetable of Activities:

TIME FRAME (BY WEEK/BY DAY)

(Day 1)   Assign roles and deadlines

(Day 5)   Brief written report outlining character, research sources, amount of time expended, questions/problems

(Day 6)   Research and writing time

(Day 8)   Script preparation and rehearsal

(Day 9)   Videotaping

(Day 10) Presentation of videotape

Evaluation: The presentation will be a major valuative tool with an emphasis on the (1) effort and time involved in preparation of character; (2) thoroughness and effectiveness of research; (3) use of props and costumes to portray time period and character; (4) critical thinking skills in demonstrating understanding of character and his or her relationship to the total unit; (5) final product; (6) submission by each student of a script as well as a narrative explaining what he or she learned about the total war in researching the character.

Corollaries to Murphy's Law: As with any major unit covering a period of this much time, it is best to establish "Checkpoints" for assigned work to be done. One very effective way to handle this is to appoint a "Stage Manager" who will coordinate these activities. The Stage Manager functions as the liaison between the class and the teacher. This role can rotate from activity to activity. This is an excellent way of continuing to make students responsible for their actions and their learning. Rotating the role provides a number of students with the opportunity to learn the importance of schedules, timing, organization, and coordination.

Course: World History/Western Civilization

Length of Activity: Unit Length

Grade Level: 9–10

Unit: Ancient Greece

Topic: Socrates/Philosophy

Title: Death of Socrates

Description of Activity:

(Circle one)

~~Documentary~~ News Report   Interview   Thought Question

Overview: This unit-length videotaped documentary activity is designed to run concurrently with a unit covering Ancient Greece. Work on the activity should take place during designated times and is meant to supplement what is taking place in class. The final product is expected to be approximately 60 minutes long in videotape form.

Number of Students: 20

List of Roles: Socrates, 2 students of Socrates, 2 accusers, 2 citizens of Athens, 1 Athenian general, 1 Athenian soldier, 2 Spartan soldiers, 2 script writers-editors, 2-person video taping crew, 3 staff researchers, 2 persons serving as art/costume designers

Concepts:
1. The need for a society to respond to self-critique, which may be seen as unpatriotic and weakening the "moral fiber" of the society and a threat to the government in power

2. The idea of truth that is greater than that which is merely relative and pertinent to the current time

3. The distinction between issues and principles and that issues can be compromised but principles cannot

Factual Information: Socrates, issue, Athens, principle, sophist, Sparta, Plato, The Republic, direct democracy, tyranny, representative democracy, Aristophanes, Peloponnesian War, Pericles, Athenian education, Spartan education, Peloponnesian League, Delian League, aristocracy, oligarchy, monarchy, Zeus, Athena, Apollo, philosophy, Helots

Skills:
1. Historical research
2. Costume design
3. Video taping
4. Learning the Socratic dialogue
5. Presentation skills

6. Self- and group evaluation skills

7. Cooperative and collaborative work

Timetable of Activities:

TIME FRAME (BY WEEK/BY DAY)

(Days 1–4)   Decide roles, begin small group assignments

(Days 5–7)   Library research and use of other sources

(Days 8–10)   Costume design, taping scheduled, initial outline

(Days 11–12)   Taping begins, students continue to refine parts

(Days 13–14)   Taping continues, final takes begin

(Days 15–18)   Production is completed, taping completed

(Days 19–21)   Group edit, completion of final product

(Days 22–25)   Presentation of final product, evaluation

Evaluation: Evaluation will be based on the presentation. Emphasis will be placed on the accuracy of research, the creativity and freshness of presentation, the amount of effort involved, the thoughtfulness of the presentation, the use of costumes and props, and the seriousness of the final presentation. Student evaluation of their own work is also a very important aspect of this production. To this end students will complete a worksheet explaining the knowledge they have gained.

Corollaries to Murphy's Law: The activity must be held to a schedule or it can ruin long-range plans. The teacher needs to develop a good working relationship with the "media specialist" in the school. Attendance should be part of the evaluation, though the people not in school should not affect those who are in school.

Course:	Social Studies
Length of Activity:	One week
Grade Level:	9–12
Unit:	World War II
Topic:	The Holocaust
Title:	Man's Inhumanity to Man

Description of Activity:

(Circle one)

~~Documentary~~   News Report   Interview   Thought Question

Overview: Perhaps no single event of the twentieth century has generated the horror, the fear, and the guilt of the Holocaust. Yet there are those who would claim it never happened; it is a giant lie. However, as history demonstrates, humankind's ability to torture and destroy our fellow humans appears to have no boundaries. Consequently, it is important that students discover not only that the holocaust happened but that Hitler came close to achieving his vision of the genocide of an entire people.

Number of Students: 20

List of Roles: Announcer, Adolf Hitler, Dr. Josef Mengele, Adolf Eichmann, Reinhard Heydrich, an SS officer, a member of the Gestapo, Anne Frank's father, three survivors of the death camps (a man, a woman, a child), a German citizen who lived near a concentration camp, five interviewers/newscasters, an American soldier who liberated the camp, two videographers

Concepts:
1. Our inhumanity to one another
2. Genocide
3. War guilt
4. Humans' ability to survive
5. Racism

Factual Information: Adolf Hitler, Adolf Eichmann, Reinhard Heydrich, Josef Mengele, the "final solution," Kristallnacht, Mein Kampf, Aryan superiority, six million Jews, Auschwitz, extreme nationalism, Gestapo, the SS, *The Diary of Anne Frank*

Skills:
1. Interviewing techniques
2. Researching skills
3. Note taking

4. Videotaping and editing

5. Map skills

6. Historical relationships

Timetable of Activities:

TIME FRAME (BY WEEK/BY DAY)

(Day 1)   Assigning roles, beginning research

(Day 2)   Continuing research

(Day 3)   Preparing script

(Day 4)   Rehearsing

(Day 5)   Videotaping

(Day 6)   Presentation and evaluation

Evaluation: Evaluation will be based on the presentation, with an emphasis on the depth and scope of research, the accuracy and props used in the presentation, the amount of effort involved, cooperation within the group, and a one-page paper on "Three things I learned in this production about our inhumanity to one another."

Corollaries to Murphy's Law: The amount of time involved in this type of activity demands attendance from all students. In any activity, when everyone has a role, it is very important that students see how their role is interrelated to that of every other participant. Additionally, the research material must be readily available in the classroom or in the library.

Course:	World Geography
Length of Activity:	One Week
Grade Level:	7–8
Unit:	Africa South of the Sahara
Topic:	Loss of Arable Land
Title:	A Village Deals with Desertification

Description of Activity:

(Circle one)

~~Documentary~~   News Report   Interview   Thought Question

Overview: This week-long activity is part of a larger unit covering Africa south of the Sahara Desert. The focus of the unit is on understanding the interrelationships between society's needs, climate, and the earth's resources. It is based on an interview of farmers by a United Nations Fact Finding team. At the end of the activity the United Nations team gives a report of their interviews conducted with the farmers, and the farmers give a report of their meeting with the United Nation's team. This strategy is meant to complement a larger unit and is planned for twenty minutes of a fifty-minute class.

Number of Students: 20

List of Roles: Ten members of a village living in a country bordering the Sahara Desert, ten members of a United Nations team representing three "western nations" charged with reporting on the conditions resulting from desertification

Concepts:
1. Desertification
2. Interdependence
3. Relationships between humans and the earth.

Factual Information: Desertification, Sahara Desert, Sahel, Chad, Knowledge of a map of Africa south of the Sahara, WHO

Skills:
1. Researching
2. Interviewing
3. Reporting

Timetable of Activities:

TIME FRAME (BY WEEK/BY DAY)

(Day 1)   Assign/select roles. Begin research

(Day 2)   Continue research

(Day 3)   Research completed, begin interviews

(Day 4)   Complete interviews, begin team meetings

(Day 5)   Complete team meetings, delivery of final report

Evaluation: Evaluation will be by the group on each of the individual interviews. Emphasis will be placed on the seriousness of the effort, the use of props, and students' creativity in presenting the material.

Corollaries to Murphy's Law: This is a strategy that has worked five times. With junior high students this activity has been exciting and productive. Drawbacks result if students are not in school at critical times.

Course:	American Studies
Length of Activity:	Ten weeks
Grade Level:	7–12
Unit:	American Revolution
Topic:	African Americans Respond to the American Revolution
Title:	An American Dilemma

Description of Activity:

(Circle one)

(Documentary) News Report Interview Thought Question

Overview: This student-produced radio documentary describes the feelings of African Americans about the Revolution that was taking place in the thirteen colonies. It is designed to take place as the class studies the American Revolution and to serve as an enrichment activity.

Number of Students: 20

List of Roles: Slaves from four southern colonies, slave owners from four southern colonies serving at the Continental Congress, one member of the Congress not in favor of slavery, four freed African Americans living as freemen, three documentary researchers, two reporters, one assistant, one program manager

Concepts:

1. The compromise enacted at the Continental Congress and later Constitutional Convention and its effect on American society

2. The differences between the perspectives of African American and white Americans during the eighteenth century concerning "life, liberty, and the pursuit of happiness"

Factual Information: Declaration of Independence, Thomas Jefferson, Benjamin Franklin, John Adams, Continental Congress, Constitutional Convention, slavery, master, freedman

Skills:

1. Interviewing

2. Being interviewed

3. Audio taping

4. Preparing and presenting an audiotape

5. Researching

Timetable of Activities:

TIME FRAME (BY WEEK/BY DAY)

(Week 1)   Selecting roles, begin research

(Week 2)   Preparation of program outline

(Week 3)   Research completes as interviewing begins

(Week 4)   Interviewing

(Week 5)   Interviewing completed

(Week 6)   Editing audiotape begins

(Week 7)   Editing completed

(Week 8)   Final product preview draft

(Weeks 9, 10) Final product and evaluation

Evaluation: Weekly evaluation by students, weekly project assessment by students, presentation of final product, evaluation of product

Corollaries to Murphy's Law:

1. Need to have someone lead a small workshop on radio and audio taping procedures.

2. When Joe Nowicki did this someone misplaced the final tape with two days left.

Course: World History/Western Civilizations

Length of Activity: One week

Grade Level: 9–10

Unit: Ancient History

Topic: Egypt

Title: Life on the Nile

Description of Activity:

(Circle one)

(Documentary) News Report   Interview   Thought Question

Overview: This documentary, designed to last a week and take the maximum class time available, is set in ancient Egypt. The activity follows a week of studying ancient Egypt. In the strategy, a film crew is sent back in time to Egypt with instructions to return with a documentary for a modern high school social studies' class.

Number of Students: 22

List of Roles: Three-person video crew, Pharaoh, two members of the royal family, two researchers, three members of a middle class Egyptian family, three members of an upper class Egyptian family, three workers on the pyramids, a Nile River boatman, a high priest, the Pharaoh's adviser, two visitors from Mesopotamia

Concepts:
1. Civilization
2. Class structure
3. Religion
4. Social control
5. Afterlife
6. Development of society
7. Legacy

Factual Information: Nile, Aton, archeology, pharaoh, hieroglyphics, Ramses II, Hatshepsut, scribes, vizier, map of Egypt and the Mediterranean world

Skills:
1. Video production and taping
2. Researching
3. Costume design
4. Mapping

5. Presenting information

6. Interviewing

Timetable of Activities:

TIME FRAME (BY WEEK/BY DAY)

(Day 1) Begin research, video crew prepares schedule

(Day 2) Researching continues, video crew provides background and script writing for reporters

(Day 3) Research completed

(Day 4) Filming of documentary

(Day 5) Presentation of documentary and evaluation

Evaluation: Student self- and peer evaluation form. Students write a reaction paper to strategy, teacher evaluation of presentation.

Corollaries to Murphy's Law: Absences hurt this activity. Students need to have roles assigned before week begins. Activity must be completed in a week or time begins to disappear.

Course: World History

Length of Activity: Seven days (Four class days, three outside)

Grade Level: 9

Unit: The Renaissance

Topic: The Great Men and Artists of the Renaissance

Title: Mona Lisa's Last Supper: The Life and Works of DaVinci

Description of Activity:

(Circle one)

(Documentary) News Report   Interview   Thought Question

Overview: Leonardo DaVinci was truly a giant of his age who left his mark on art, architecture, technology, painting, anatomy, and many other areas. He was truly a genius. A study of his life and his contemporaries will create a human picture of the man, his genius, his world, and his age. By using his works and his ideas students will gain a firsthand look at life in the Renaissance and what impact his genius had on the future. At times the class can be split into two groups, with each group preparing the same project. This gives the class a chance to have some healthy competition as well as another group with whom to share and compare ideas. This is especially effective in comparing final projects and determining what makes each special. This helps greatly in evaluation.

Number of Students: 20

List of Roles: This assignment is effective with double roles and two separate groups creating their own documentaries. However, the characters remain the same: Michelangelo, Leonardo DaVinci, Shakespeare, the model for the *Mona Lisa,* the local doctor, a modern doctor, a modern engineer, his assistant, an art historian, two researchers, two videographers, documentary host/announcer, interviewers as necessary.

Concepts:
1. What is art?
2. What is genius?
3. What is beauty?
4. How humans react to genius and beauty?

Factual Information: Renaissance, Medici, Florence, Leonardo DaVinci, Michelangelo, Raphael, Cervantes, Shakespeare, individualism, perspective, balance and proportion, tempera, frescoes, *The Last Supper, The Mona Lisa*

Skills:	1. Research
	2. Cooperative effort and interdependence
	3. Adopting historical persona
	4. Scripting
	5. Videotaping principles
	6. Oral presentation skills

Timetable of Activities:

TIME FRAME (BY WEEK/BY DAY)

(Day 1)	Explain and assign roles; begin research
(Day 2)	Library research day
(Day 3)	Work continues outside of class
(Day 4)	Each student submits an outline of work accomplished; work continues outside of class
(Day 5)	Class time for rehearsal and preparation
(Day 6)	Class time for videotaping
(Day 7)	Viewing of videotaping

Evaluation: Final presentation with an emphasis on the written outline from each student, the depth of research, the seriousness of the development of each historical persona, the overall quality of the documentary, and the accuracy of the final picture of Leonardo and his age.

Corollaries to Murphy's Law: Two of the biggest considerations are time and absenteeism. As with many of these productions, things only work when the people are there to make them work. If people are absent then the rest of the group will suffer unless they make some rather heroic individual efforts. Consequently, it is important to establish some sort of system for recognizing the efforts of the students who come to class.

Course:	World History
Length of Activity:	Three days
Grade Level:	9
Unit:	World War I
Topic:	The Personal War—At Home and at the Front
Title:	A Day in the Life of: (a German citizen; an American soldier in training; a French factory worker; the girlfriend of a London soldier; a German schoolteacher; a French shopkeeper)

Description of Activity:

(Circle one)

Documentary ⟨News Report⟩ Interview   Thought Question

Overview: For students to develop a strong idea of war, it is important to flesh out the historical statistics with people reacting to the very real situations that the war has created. Effective accomplishment of this task requires a lesson on the emotional impact the war has on the people, both at home and in the front lines.

Number of Students: 20

List of Roles: A German soldier, a French soldier fighting in his homeland, an English soldier, an American doughboy, a young wife and mother in France, a German soldier's mother and father, the owner of a small grocery store in France, a policeman in Berlin, a history teacher in England

Concepts:
1. The humanity in war
2. The human toll of war
3. The universal impact of war

Factual Information: Rationing, propaganda, technology, industrialization, trench warfare, no man's land, the draft, role of women (feminism), casualty lists, sniper, Battle of Verdun, *All Quiet on the Western Front,* Eastern Front, Western Front, the Lusitania, U-Boats, Zimmermann letter

Skills:
1. Inferential thinking skills
2. Research skills
3. First person persona to subjectify historical data
4. Questioning skills

Timetable of Activities:

TIME FRAME (BY WEEK/BY DAY)

(Day 1)   Assign roles and begin research

(Day 2)   Research and writing

(Day 3)   Presentations

Evaluation: Evaluation will be based on the presentation. Emphasis will be placed on the accuracy of research, the creativity or freshness of presentation, the amount of effort involved, the thoughtfulness of the presentation.

Corollaries to Murphy's Law: Time and absenteeism are both major factors. Students have to be in school for the activity. Although any absent students can turn the report into a paper or an audiotape, or even present their activity after school, the effect is not the same.

Course: World History

Length of Activity: Five days

Grade Level: 9

Unit: The Middle Ages

Topic: The Magna Carta

Title: The Evening News—A Report from Runnymeade

Description of Activity:

(Circle one)

Documentary ⟨News Report⟩ Interview   Thought Question

Overview: The signing of the Magna Carta is one of those events of such historical significance that it would be surrounded by a media blitz were it to occur in today's communication age. Consequently, this type of event can be best brought to life in the evening news format in which the signing is witnessed followed by analysis and commentary from experts, eyewitnesses, and the average Middle Ages citizen.

Number of Students: 20

List of Roles: News anchor, two reporters from the scene, King John, Baron Robert Fitzwalter, a second Baron, Stephen Langton, Pope Innocent III, one of the King John's supporters, King John's sheriff, a serf on the manor, his wife, a wife of a baron, a journeyman, an apprentice, a lady of the castle, a woman on the manor, two videographers, a researcher

Concepts:
1. The evolution of English common law
2. The jury system: grand jury, jury trials
3. Limits of power of monarchs/rulers
4. The principles involved in fair taxation

Factual Information: Magna Carta, Pope Innocent III, Stephen Langton, King John, English Common Law, Runnymeade, 1215, absolute monarchy, limited monarchy, parliament, serfs, barons, feudal system

Skills:
1. Library research skills
2. Map reading skills (Runnymeade)
3. Writing/speaking in the first-person persona
4. Creating open-ended questions

Timetable of Activities:

TIME FRAME (BY WEEK/BY DAY)

(Day 1)   Assign roles and define terms

(Day 2)   Research and preparation of roles

(Day 3)   Creation of scripts

(Day 4)   Rehearsal

(Day 5)   Presentation of newscast

Evaluation: The evaluation will consist of the presentation with special emphasis on the degree of preparation, thoroughness of research, accuracy of presentation, use of props and costumes, quality of interviews, seriousness of presentation, amount of effort.

Corollaries to Murphy's Law: One of the major points to be wary of in this type of activity is that the students sometimes become obsessed with one part of the production and loose sight of the historical part. Do not let them become so involved in props and costumes that they spend all of their time on that part and shortchange the historical data.

Course:	World History
Length of Activity:	Three days
Grade Level:	9
Unit:	The Age of Absolute Power and Revolution
Topic:	The French Revolution
Title:	The Reign of Terror

Description of Activity:

(Circle one)

Documentary   (News Report)   Interview   Thought Question

Overview: To understand revolution, students must look at the Reign of Terror as an excess of the second phase of revolution, as the king is killed and the power is in the hands of the radicals. At this point the newscast is a quick and enjoyable way to cover a large topic in a short, efficient, and effective activity.

Number of Students: 20

List of Roles: News anchor desk, four correspondents on the scene, Louis XVI, Marie Antoinette, Maximillian de Robespierre, Napoleon Bonaparte, Jean Paul Marat, Georges Danton, the executioner, a guard at the Bastille, Thomas Jefferson, the mother of the young man who was executed for cutting down the "liberty" tree, a French nobleman, his wife, two peasants

Concepts:
1. The three stages of revolution
2. Abuses of power
3. Revolution as an adjunct of nationalism
4. Classed society

Factual Information: Three estates, Estates General, Louis XVI, Marie Antoinette, Jacobins, Bastille, Jean Paul Marat, Robespierre, Reign of Terror, Great Fear, Guillotine, Girondists, Danton, Directory, Sans Culottes, Levee en Masse, "Liberty, Equality and Fraternity," Napoleon, Louis XV, Bourgeois, Tennis Court Oath

Skills:
1. Library research skills
2. Cooperative interdependence to complete a task
3. Leading questions
4. Inferential thought development
5. Diagramming

6. Videotaping

7. Videotape editing

8. Sequencing of events, ideas

Timetable of Activities:

TIME FRAME (BY WEEK/BY DAY)

(Day 1)   Assignment of roles and tasks

(Day 2)   Researching roles and background

(Day 3)   Writing script and rehearsing

(Day 4)   Videotaping

(Day 5)   Presentation

Evaluation: The presentation will be a major part of the evaluation, with an emphasis on (1) thoroughness and accuracy of research; (2) props, costumes, "special effects"; (3) amount of effort and involvement; (4) seriousness and effectiveness of the presentation; (5) a journal entry written by each student on "What I learned about revolution through my character and the process of researching."

Corollaries to Murphy's Law: Time is again an important factor. Time limits must be set. Generally we have found that the students perform best if strict time limits are set and followed. Occasionally problems arise that require revisions in the schedule, but that is negotiable between the "stage manager" and the teacher. If the guidelines are fair the students will stay on task. And that is one of the most important learnings—stay on task and be accountable for your responsibilities.

Course:	World History/Western Civilization
Length of Activity:	One week
Grade Level:	9–10
Unit:	Ancient History/Rome
Topic:	Julius Caesar
Title:	Reports Concerning Caesar's Death

Description of Activity:

(Circle one)

Documentary (News Report) Interview   Thought Question

Overview: Students construct a report for a "Newspaper Extra" reporting the death of Julius Caesar. The class is divided into those who represent Senators involved in the conspiracy, those opposed, and other citizens of Rome. The activity is designed to last a week and produce a "newspaper front page." The activity is designed to complement a unit.

Number of Students: 20

List of Roles: Two senators (one in favor of Caesar and one against), a Roman soldier, a Gaul, two merchants in Rome, one Roman worker, a general, Cleopatra, Octavian, a Greek, and nine reporters with one serving as an Editor-in-Chief

Concepts:
1. How a political assassination can effect a society
2. The reasons for groups opposing one another politically in society

Factual Information: Assassination, politics, senate, colonies, military society, dictatorship, democracy, republic, Spartacus, Brutus, Crassus, Pompey, Brutus, Marc Antony, Octavian, Cleopatra, the Ides of March

Skills:
1. Interviewing
2. Processing data
3. Researching roles and personages
4. Writing and presenting data
5. Organizing a "newspaper report"

Timetable of Activities:

TIME FRAME (BY WEEK/BY DAY)

(Day 1)   Assign roles, begin research

(Day 2)   Complete research

(Day 3)   Interviews begin during class time, writing begins

(Day 4)   Interviews completed, writing up interview stories

(Day 5)   Draft of interviews formatted into "newspaper"

(Day 6)   Student sharing of final draft

Evaluation: Daily teacher evaluation of student activity, daily student self- and peer evaluation according to form provided by teacher, evaluation of each product of students, evaluation and presentation of final product by students and teacher

Corollaries to Murphy's Law: All students need to be in class, and the teacher should not let time drag the activity into more than one week. Students need to know expectations and limits.

Course:	World History
Length of Activity:	Six days
Grade Level:	9
Unit:	The Reformation
Topic:	Abuses within the Church
Title:	Martin Luther and His 95 Theses

Description of Activity:

(Circle one)

Documentary ⟨News Report⟩ Interview   Thought Question

Overview: What was the impact of Martin Luther's posting of the 95 Theses on the door at Wittenburg? Luther had no intention of setting in motion the chain of events that seemed to follow his personal declaration of the state of affairs of the Catholic Church. However, this event set in motion sweeping changes and reforms that reverberated throughout the Christian world for many years. What was Martin Luther thinking? Why were his beliefs and his action so controversial and frightening to the church? We return to that historic day and see what the people then were thinking.

Number of Students: 20

List of Roles: News anchor, three correspondents, Martin Luther, a parish priest in Wittenburg, the Pope, Tetzel, Emperor Charles V, Frederick of Saxony, announcer, four students to work on commercials on the news, two videographers, three citizens of Wittenburg

Concepts:
1. The Reformation
2. Religious freedom
3. Right of dissent
4. Heresy
5. Reformation linked to spirit of renaissance

Factual Information: Martin Luther, Tetzel, Pope Leo X, Charles V—the Holy Roman Emperor, Peace of Augsburg, Protestant, Calvinism, Act of Supremacy, Wittenburg, 95 Theses, Charles V, Frederick of Saxony, John Calvin, John Knox

Skills:
1. Interviewing techniques
2. Videotaping and editing
3. Researching
4. Adopting historical persona

5. Map skills

6. Critical thinking skills

Timetable of Activities:

TIME FRAME (BY WEEK/BY DAY)

(Day 1)   Assigning roles and beginning research

(Day 2)   Researching roles

(Day 3)   Preparing scripts

(Day 4)   Rehearsal

(Day 5)   Videotaping

(Day 6)   Presentation

Evaluation: The evaluation will be based on the effectiveness of the newscast. Special emphasis will be placed on thoroughness of research, accuracy of research, seriousness of effort, amount of time, effectiveness of questions, and completeness of answers. Students also will complete one-page essays on their roles and what they learned.

Corollaries to Murphy's Law: The coordination and maintenance of the time schedule are very important. Failure to have both of these areas tight can create a number of problems.

Course:	American Studies
Length of Activity:	Two days
Grade Level:	10–12
Unit:	Past Elections in the United States
Topic:	Issues Concerning Voters
Title:	A Look Back to the Election of (*fill in the year*)

Description of Activity:

(Circle one)

Documentary (News Report) Interview   Thought Question

Overview: This two-day "news cast" is designed to provide a comparison of today's issues with those pressing the country during some past election held in the nineteenth century. The teacher and students decide to focus on one election representing the topic area under study. Fifteen students become "person on the street" interviews for a group of five interviewers. Those interviewed must describe themselves for the audience. The interviews will be audio taped and replayed as a radio broadcast. The group focuses on issues current during the designated election.

Number of Students: 20

List of Roles: Five interviewers/reporters, fifteen citizens (students choose particulars) one would expect to have found "on the street" in their town during this particular election

Concepts:
1. Elections reflect public opinion
2. How some issues change over time yet others remain constant

Factual Information: Choice of five issues particular to an election, knowledge of a particular election, development of characters common to a time in the past and knowledge of their attitudes

Skills:
1. Audio taping
2. Researching
3. Developing characters and scripts
4. Presentation of information

**Timetable of
Activities:**

TIME FRAME (BY WEEK/BY DAY)

(Day 1)   Taping begins, research ongoing as homework

(Day 2)   Taping complete on a 20-minute tape

(Day 3)   Students complete a reaction paper for homework

Evaluation: Evaluation of final production, student self-evaluation, student peer evaluation, teacher evaluation of product, teacher evaluation of reaction paper

**Corollaries to
Murphy's Law:**   The first time this exercise bombed because students could not understand how to develop the role of an ordinary "person in the street" from an earlier time. It is beneficial if the class, as a group, sets the agenda about what issues it expects everyone to focus on. At this point the teacher may need to show the class how issues do involve all of us.

Course:	American Studies
Length of Activity:	Five days
Grade Level:	10–12
Unit:	Reconstruction
Topic:	Impeachment of Andrew Johnson
Title:	Reports from the Congress

Description of Activity:

(Circle one)

Documentary ⟨**News Report and Interview**⟩ Thought Question

Overview: This activity is designed to increase an understanding of the political debate that fractured the presidency of Andrew Johnson. Five student reporters are to interview ten students representing particular members of congress. Five voted to save Johnson and five voted against. The reports will be presented in a newspaper format from the time. Additionally, all students will write a "letter to the editor" about the issue, and five will be "published."

Number of Students: 18

List of Roles: Five members of Congress pro-Johnson, five against Johnson, five reporters, three students as newspaper editors

Concepts:
1. The impact of politics on U.S. government
2. The divisions left after the Civil War

Factual Information: Andrew Johnson, votes of particular people in Congress, reconstruction, radical Republicans

Skills:
1. Developing the persona of someone from the past
2. Developing an understanding of a particular issue
3. Interviewing
4. Reporting
5. Presenting a particular position by letter
6. Developing a newspaper

Timetable of Activities:

TIME FRAME (BY WEEK/BY DAY)

(Day 1)   Assign roles; all students begin research

(Day 2)   Interviews begin

(Day 3)   Interviews conclude

(Day 4)   Letters to editor due

(Day 5)   Editors complete final layout for class, copies distributed to all

Evaluation: Student self- and peer evaluation from sheets, teacher evaluation of daily experience, evaluation of final product

Corollaries to Murphy's Law: Use entire class time for one week. Editors must understand that layout work may require extra efforts outside of class.

Course:	American Studies
Length of Activity:	One day
Grade Level:	10–12
Unit:	The Sixties
Topic:	The Assassination of John F. Kennedy
Title:	Where Were You When Kennedy Was Killed?

Description of Activity:

(Circle one)

Documentary   News Report   Interview   ⟨Thought Question⟩

Overview: It is very important for students to recognize that certain events occur that historically have tremendous influence on people. Events such as the assassination of Kennedy was such an event. It becomes a moment by which people look at history on a personal level. Consequently, we see history as people, not simply as facts and data.

Number of Students: 20

List of Roles: All students function as interviewers

Concepts:
1. Historical chance
2. Individual reactions to historical events
3. Impact of historical events on society

Factual Information: The events in Dallas, Texas, on November 22, 1963

Skills: Interviewing and transcription skills

Timetable of Activities:

TIME FRAME (BY WEEK/BY DAY)

(Day 1)   Presented as one-day homework assignment

Evaluation: Student presentation of the information they have gained in the interview and the one-page transcription submitted to the teacher.

Corollaries to Murphy's Law: Keeping students to the one page, especially on this question, presents a challenge. Many of their parents are of an age where they remember exactly what they were doing. Consequently, they tend to want to talk forever about it.

Course:	World History
Length of Activity:	One day
Grade Level:	9
Unit:	World War I
Topic:	War
Title:	Is War Ever Justifiable?

Description of Activity:

(Circle one)

Documentary   News Report   Interview   (Thought Question)

Overview: The purpose of this assignment is to have students probe the reactions of other people to thought questions that are often controversial in nature. This activity allows students to learn about a topic in a nonthreatening way while hearing other people's impressions before they have to "stand and deliver" their own ideas. It allows students time to consider their idea and to compare it with that of other people. This helps students to further amplify and develop opinions and relate to larger events within the society.

Number of Students: 20

List of Roles: Questioners

Concepts: 1. War—what is it all about?

Factual Information: Varies with the answers students get.

Skills:
1. Critical questioning
2. Transcription skills
3. Forming relationships of ideas

Timetable of Activities:

TIME FRAME (BY WEEK/BY DAY)

(Day 1)   Assign question for homework; discuss in class next day

Evaluation: Students will write a one-page summary of their findings.

Corollaries to Murphy's Law: Some students will ask people who go on forever or who answer in one or two words. In making the assignment, stress that the answers are limited to one page.

Course: World History/United States History

Length of Activity: One day

Grade Level: 8–10

Unit: The Age of Absolute Power and Revolution

Topic: Causes of Revolution

Title: Is America Ripe for a Revolution Today?

Description of Activity:

(Circle one)

Documentary News Report Interview **Thought Question**

Overview: To keep students looking at the practical applications of the study of history, it is important to continually have them attempt to make comparisons between earlier stages of history and contemporary history. Revolution is with us today in many third world countries. However, to fire their imaginations and to look closely at the lessons of history, it is important to mirror the concepts of revolution to the United States today. How well do they know or understand what is happening today? Does it fit into an historical context? These are questions that this thought question will stimulate.

Number of Students: 20

List of Roles: Interviewers and interviewee

Concepts:
1. Causes of revolution
2. Cycle of history

Factual Information: Three stages of revolution

Skills:
1. Interviewing techniques
2. Transcription
3. Ability to distinguish cause and effect
4. Summarizing

Timetable of Activities:

TIME FRAME (BY WEEK/BY DAY)

(Day 1) Assign as homework

(Day 2) Report to the class

Evaluation: Students will write a one-page narration highlighting the interviewee's observations and insights. A final paragraph will reflect the students' personal feelings about the comments.

Corollaries to Murphy's Law: Some students will interview parents who will talk forever on the subject; others will get one- or two-word answers. Stress to the class a one-page summary.

Course: World History/Western Civilization

Length of Activity: One day

Grade Level: 9–10

Unit: Ancient Civilizations/Rome

Topic: Julius Caesar

Title: Do We Need a Caesar Type of Leader in Our Society?

Description of Activity:

(Circle one)

Documentary   News Report   Interview   (Thought Question)

Overview: This one-day Thought Question asks students to evaluate their world in terms of the leadership model offered by Julius Caesar to the Romans and to apply that model of leadership to the world of today. Students are required to interview one adult and report on that interview.

Number of Students: 25–30

List of Roles: Students as interviewers

Concepts:

1. Issues of leadership and governing social life can be similar over time.

2. Many societies have faced similar problems.

Factual Information: Spartacus, Julius Caesar, Brutus, First Triumvirate, Optimates, Populares, Tiberius Gracchus, Gaul, dictator, senate

Skills:

1. Students as interviewers

2. Transcription

3. Presentation

Timetable of Activities:

TIME FRAME (BY WEEK/BY DAY)

(Day 1)   Students ask Thought Question as an overnight assignment.

Evaluation: Student presentation of data to class and teacher evaluation of student-written transcripts and reactions.

Corollaries to Murphy's Law: Those interviewed by students need to consider alternatives to their current system of governance.

Course: World History/Western Civilization

Length of Activity: One day

Grade Level: 9–10

Unit: Age of Discovery/Exploration

Topic: Traveling with an Explorer

Title: Would You Go to Planet X?

Description of Activity:

(Circle one)

Documentary   News Report   Interview   ⟨Thought Question⟩

Overview: Students are asked to respond to this thought question and "interview themselves." They are to assume that the United States Government has selected them to take part in the first human trip to Planet X in a distant galaxy. The trip will take thirty years. The explorers are expected to remain long enough to decide if the planet is suitable for colonization. The student-explorers will then return to Earth. Ninth or tenth graders are selected to go because of their age. There is no guarantee of return, but a successful return would ensure wealth and security. Would the students go on such a trip if offered the chance?

Number of Students: 25–30

List of Roles: N/A

Concepts:
1. The idea of the unknown in exploration
2. The commonality faced by all explorers
3. The reasons for and for not going on a venture of exploration
4. Understanding the fears faced by early explorers

Factual Information: Marco Polo, Drake, Dias, Prince Henry, Christopher Columbus (among many other explorers)

Skills:
1. Application of concepts to current life
2. Writing and presenting skills

Timetable of Activities:

TIME FRAME (BY WEEK/BY DAY)

(Day 1)   Students present their opinions the next day in class

Evaluation: Student presentation and teacher evaluation of one-page reaction papers

Corollaries to
Murphy's Law: All or none of the students may opt for either going to Planet X or remaining behind on Earth.

Course:	World History/Western Civilization
Length of Activity:	One day
Grade Level:	9–10
Unit:	Industrial Revolution
Topic:	Technology
Title:	Thought Question: Does Technology Always Improve Life?

Description of Activity:

(Circle one)

Documentary   News Report   Interview   ⟨**Thought Question**⟩

Overview: This one-day Thought Question exercise is designed to run with the classroom discussion of the alterations in society caused by the Industrial Revolution of the nineteenth century. Students are required to interview one adult and to report the results to the class the next day. As with all Thought Questions, students are required to transcribe the answers to their interview questions and turn in this sheet as a part of their homework assignment.

Number of Students: 20–25

List of Roles: Students as interviewers

Concepts:
1. The idea that technological change can foster social change
2. Technological and social change are as rapid today as at any time in our past

Factual Information: Industrial Revolution, utopia, socialism, capitalism, Luddites, Thomas Malthus, Enclosure Movement

Skills:
1. Interviewing
2. Data processing

Timetable of Activities:

TIME FRAME (BY WEEK/BY DAY)

(Day 1)   Students complete interviews for homework assignment.

Evaluation: Student presentation of interviews to class, teacher evaluation of transcripts collected at the end of class

Corollaries to
Murphy's Law: Adults refusing to respond to students can impair student success during the activity.

Course: World History/Western Civilization

Length of Activity: One day

Grade Level: 9–12

Unit: Napoleonic France

Topic: Napoleon's Reform Based Belief in a National Education Policy

Title: Should the United States Establish a National Curriculum?

Description of Activity:

(Circle one)

Documentary   News Report   Interview   ⟨Thought Question⟩

Overview: This one-day Thought Question is planned to supplement a larger activity dealing with Napoleon. It seeks to link the ideas of Napoleon with the world of today for students. Students are asked to interview one person over the age of 21 and one of their peers from outside the class. They are to report the results the next day.

Number of Students: 25–30

List of Roles: Students as interviewers

Concepts:
1. School curriculum used as a means of directing personal and moral opinions in society
2. Education as a means for social control
3. The autonomy and freedom provided by local control of education

Factual Information: Autonomy, mandate, social control, Napoleon, domestic policy, local control of education, national curriculum, national teacher testing and hiring

Skills:
1. Interviewing
2. Questioning
3. Processing data
4. Presenting data

Timetable of Activities:

TIME FRAME (BY WEEK/BY DAY)

(Day 1)   Assigned one day and presented the next

Evaluation: Student presentation of data, teacher evaluation of written material collected at the end of presentation class

Corollaries to
Murphy's Law: Adults and peers may not wish to respond or may respond in too great a detail for a one-page assignment.

Course:	History
Length of Activity:	One day
Grade Level:	9–12
Unit:	World War II
Topic:	The War with Japan
Title:	The Dropping of the Bombs

Description of Activity:

(Circle one)

Documentary   News Report   Interview   ⟨Thought Question⟩

Overview: A topic that has always generated controversy was President Harry Truman's decision to drop the atomic bomb on Japan. Today the United States remains the only nation in the world to use such a weapon of mass destruction. A thought question on the morality of this decision is a very powerful tool to involve students in the sides of this issue. However, to be effective this question is best asked to two different age groups. They need to ask the question of someone older than age 60 and someone between the ages of 21 and 40. This increases the possibility of differing viewpoints.

Number of Students: 20

List of Roles: All students are interviewers

Concepts:
1. The burdens of power
2. The use of force
3. Morality in war
4. Our inhumanity to one another

Factual Information: Hiroshima, Nagasaki, Harry Truman, the Enola Gay, August 6, 1945, radiation, 80,000 people killed and 37,000 injured, August 9, 1945, the Manhattan Project, August 15, 1945, Albert Einstein, Enrico Fermi, Edward Teller, Los Alamos, New Mexico, Emperor Hirohito, the Missouri

Skills:
1. Interviewing techniques
2. Transcription skills
3. Comparison and contrasting skills
4. Listening skills
5. Summarizing skills

Timetable of Activities:

TIME FRAME (BY WEEK/BY DAY)

(Day 1)   Assign question for homework

(Day 2)   Discussion and comparison of answers

Evaluation: Students submit a one- to two-page summary of their subjects' responses.

Corollaries to Murphy's Law: Students must be in school to get the assignment; otherwise they are unable to participate. One effective way to deal with the problem is to have homework buddies. The buddies are responsible for relaying all assignments to their missing buddy. On a one-night homework this works very well.

Course:	U.S. Geography
Length of Activity:	One day
Grade Level:	7–12
Unit:	Westward Migration
Topic:	What Does It Take to Move from Your Town?
Title:	Thought Question: Could You Have Left for Oregon in 1848?

Description of Activity:

(Circle one)

Documentary   News Report   Interview   (Thought Question)

Overview: As a part of the unit on migration to California, Oregon, and Utah during the 1840s, students are asked to interview an adult to find out if they would have made the trip to Oregon during the late 1840s.

Number of Students: 25–30

List of Roles: Interviewers

Concepts:
1. Migration is a very personal issue   *popular migrations during that time?*
2. Migration is motivated by factors outside of one's control
3. Migration is seen as a chance at new beginnings

Factual Information: Oregon Trail, Mountain Men, Mormons, California Trail, Donner Party, Fort Hall, Sublette Cutoff, St. Joseph, Independence Rock, Ft. Laramie, Map of the Great Plains and the Intermountain West, Sioux (Dakota), Cheyenne, Crow, Continental Divide, South Pass

Skills: Interviewing

Timetable of Activities:

TIME FRAME (BY WEEK/BY DAY)

(Day 1)   Homework assignment for one night, to be reported the next day

Evaluation: Student presentations and teacher reactions to written statements

Corollaries to Murphy's Law: Problems arise both when somebody does not do their thought question and when someone does too many pages in their transcript and wants to read their responses to the class.

Course:	World Geography
Length of Activity:	One day
Grade Level:	7–8
Unit:	East Asia–China
Topic:	Population Control/Overpopulation
Title:	Should the Government Have the Right to Control Population?

Description of Activity:

(Circle one)

Documentary   News Report   Interview   (Thought Question)

Overview: This Thought Question is set up as a one-day homework assignment. The students will interview one adult and report on their findings the next day. To verify the effort each student will turn in no longer than a one-page transcript.

Number of Students: 25–30

List of Roles: All students as interviewers

Concepts:

1. The linkage between population control and society

2. The right of the government to control population as opposed to the right of the individual to have children

Factual Information: Zero population growth, China, interdependence, social control

Skills: Interviewing, reporting

Timetable of Activities:

TIME FRAME (BY WEEK/BY DAY)

(Day 1)   Students use exercise as an overnight assignment

Evaluation: Report to class. Students also turn in transcript pages to teacher as part of a graded homework assignment.

Corollaries to Murphy's Law: Students must try to keep to the one-page limit for transcriptions. Students also may be assigned their own reaction papers for a next evening's homework assignment. This strategy should serve to reinforce work on an East Asian unit.

Course:	World History/Ancient History/Western Civilization
Length of Activity:	One day
Grade Level:	9–10
Unit:	Ancient History
Topic:	Early Civilizations/Beginnings of Society
Title:	What Does It Mean to Be Civilized?
Description of Activity:	(Circle one) Documentary News Report Interview (Thought Question)
Overview:	This Thought Question is designed as a one-day homework assignment. Students are asked to interview one person older than 21 years of age and one person younger than 21, completing a one-page transcription for each. This question will serve as a constant reference point throughout the study of Western Civilizations. It reflects one "theme" of the course.
Number of Students:	25–30
List of Roles:	All students as interviewers
Concepts:	The meaning of civilization
Factual Information:	Division of labor, technology, culture, social structure, society
Skills:	Interviewing, reporting
Timetable of Activities:	**TIME FRAME (BY WEEK/BY DAY)** (Day 1) Interviews conducted as one evening's homework
Evaluation:	Student presentation of reports, teacher evaluation of student transcripts
Corollaries to Murphy's Law:	This question is used to frame a course and can be re-asked throughout the length of the course. On this question no student should be allowed to escape this exercise. This is a recurring thought, and students need to have a foundation from which to build.

Course: American Studies

Length of Activity: Two days

Grade Level: 9–11

Unit: The Civil War

Topic: The Individual in War

Title: The Letter: Is the War Worth the Sacrifice and Suffering?

Description of Activity:

(Circle one)

Documentary   News Report   Interview   (Thought Question)

Overview: Students are asked to respond to this question by interviewing themselves about the impact of war on the life of a particular person during the Civil War. Through this activity the students are required to put themselves into a particular role and then share their deepest feelings about personal commitment in a letter to a loved one at home or in the war. The activity demands that students carefully examine issues such as morality and values, both societal and those of the individual.

Number of Students: 20–25

List of Roles: Young soldier at the front (either Union or Confederate), young nurse tending the wounded, a girlfriend or wife at home, a mother or father at home

Concepts:
1. Wars are fought by people
2. People are expendable in war
3. Hardships of war
4. Personal commitment to ideals and values

Factual Information: Any material from the unit that the student has previously studied or any new material the student discovers in the researching of the topic

Skills:
1. Interviewing techniques
2. Assuming historical persona
3. Applying historical roles to personal ideals
4. Writing personal essay
5. Presentation to class

Timetable of Activities:

TIME FRAME (BY WEEK/BY DAY)

(Day 1) Selecting roles and researching

(Day 2) Presentation

Evaluation: Student presentation and teacher reaction to the written letter. Special attention will be given to historical accuracy of supporting detail, believability of material, seriousness of effort, and accurate characterization of role.

Corollaries to Murphy's Law: Although two days are given for this exercise, it is best to give the students about two to three days to work on the letter outside of class. It is a nice supporting assignment while studying the battles of the Civil War and the cost in human lives and suffering. Kerry found that a very good follow-up for this activity is to tie it to the Reconstruction unit. After they see the results and the failures of Reconstruction, have them reread their letters and then react to the ideas they expressed earlier.

Course:	U.S. Government
Length of Activity:	One day
Grade Level:	10–12
Unit:	Constitution
Topic:	Bill of Rights
Title:	Respond to (Any of the Issues Raised in the First Amendment)

Description of Activity:

(Circle one)

Documentary News Report Interview ⟨Thought Question⟩

Overview: This Thought Question can be used to explore any issue raised by the First Amendment.

Number of Students: 25–30

List of Roles: Each student conducts an interview with one person older than age 21 and one person younger than age 21.

Concepts: Freedom's expression in the document that guides our society

Factual Information: Knowledge of First Amendment

Skills:
1. Interviewing
2. Reporting
3. Applying First Amendment to daily life

Timetable of Activities:

TIME FRAME (BY WEEK/BY DAY)

(Day 1)   Thought Question as one-day homework assignment.

Evaluation: Student presentation of information, teacher evaluation of written transcripts

Corollaries to Murphy's Law: Be prepared: Reactions can become controversial!

Course:	World History
Length of Activity:	Two days
Grade Level:	10–12
Unit:	World War II
Topic:	Effects of War on People, Soldiers and Civilians
Title:	Personal Memoirs

Description of Activity:

(Circle one)

Documentary   News Report   (Interview)   Thought Question

Overview: This activity is designed to increase an understanding of the personal side of war, to probe the reactions of other people to personal events with historical meaning, and to give students a stronger sense of primary research using nonthreatening methodology. Students are to interview a grandparent or some other adult who was alive during World War II and has memories of the war either as a participant or on the home front. The interview must be audiotaped or videotaped for future reference. Students will begin with four to five basic questions such as: Where were you on December 7, 1941? What do you remember about the war? What do you remember about V-E Day? What do you remember about V-J Day? What did you think when you learned about the dropping of the atomic bomb? Students will be required to videotape or audiotape their responses. Students will then transcribe the material into hard copy for submission into a class-created text of World War II personal memoirs from their families and acquaintances.

Number of Students: 20–25

List of Roles: Interviewer and interviewee

Concepts:
1. War is real
2. War is current
3. War affects people
4. War is personal
5. People make history

Factual Information: World War II, atomic bombs, Pearl Harbor, European Theater, Pacific Theater, V-E Day, V-J Day, personal facts from interviewee

Skills:
1. Interviewing/questioning techniques
2. Audio/videotaping

3. Presentation of material

4. Transcribing oral material into text

Timetable of Activities:

TIME FRAME (BY WEEK/BY DAY)

(Day 1)   Explain assignment

(Day 2)   Present material to class

Evaluation: Student presentation of material to class, teacher evaluation of the written transcript, peer evaluation of the nature and depth of questioning, seriousness of interview

Corollaries to Murphy's Law: Some problems might occur if the grandparents live out of town or if grandparents are not available for interviewing. Some students are very creative in taping, for example, using telephone answering machines for long-distance interviews, but this can be expensive for some students. Teachers should develop a list of resources, some of whom may be found right in the school, to help those students without relatives. Additionally, because a quality interview takes some time, we have found the students need at least a weekend just for the logistics. Teachers should give the students about a week for the interview and a few days beyond the interview for the completion of the transcripts. We have had some interviews last 35 to 40 minutes; others, 3 to 5 hours. Factors such as scope, editing, and final presentation of the interview need to be discussed with students. Remind students that for some of the adults this can be painful but rewarding. Some of our students have discovered they have relatives who were truly heroic.

Course:	American Studies
Length of Activity:	Three days
Grade Level:	9–12
Unit:	The Civil War
Topic:	Abraham Lincoln's Leadership
Title:	The President's Speech: A Report from Gettysburg

Description of Activity:

(Circle one)

Documentary ⟨News Report⟩ Interview   Thought Question

Overview: This news report is designed as a part of the unit on the Civil War and shows the impact of the war through the larger conceptual directions that are changed by war. The Gettysburg Address is an example of a speech that clearly demonstrated the loftier ideals Lincoln was attaching to the sacrifice of men in battle. Additionally, it is important for students to see the context in which the speech was delivered and the reaction of the people of the time as they draw comparisons with contemporary events and reactions. This activity can stand on its own as a newscast or can easily be incorporated as a segment of the evening news.

Number of Students: 12

List of Roles: Abraham Lincoln, news anchor, two field reporters, a union army officer who fought at Gettysburg, a nurse who has been tending the wounded, two Union soldiers who were wounded in the battle, the mother of a wounded solder, the wife of a soldier killed at Gettysburg, a United States senator, Secretary of War Edwin Stanton

Concepts:
1. Impact of war
2. How a president's speech impacts policy
3. Individual reactions to historical events
4. Determining character from ideals and values
5. How people make history

Factual Information: Lincoln, Battle of Gettysburg, the Gettysburg Cemetery dedication ceremony, Declaration of Independence, preamble to the Constitution

Skills:
1. Inferential thinking
2. Research skills
3. First-person persona

4. Questioning techniques

5. Analysis of language

6. Recognizing cause and effect relationships

Timetable of Activities:

TIME FRAME (BY WEEK/BY DAY)

(Day 1)   Assign roles and begin researching

(Day 2)   Researching

(Day 3)   Researching and script writing

(Day 4)   Presentation

Evaluation: Emphasis on accuracy and depth of research, creativity and freshness of presentation, amount of effort and seriousness of the presentation, written scripts and student summary of "What I learned. . . ."

Corollaries to Murphy's Law: Absenteeism and time remain important factors. Pairing of students and assigning of characters is very important, especially because some of the activities require a greater degree of inference than others. With this type of activity it is important at some point to do some inferential skill development work in the area of the thoughts and feelings of the "common man." It is helpful to have, as we have mentioned earlier, a librarian and strong supporting research material.

CHAPTER 4

The Demonstration

The demonstration is a learning and teaching strategy that is familiar to all students and educators. It has been around for as long as teachers have asked students to share what they have learned with others. In the early grades teachers called it "show and tell," the golden opportunity for eager learners to share their knowledge with peers and teachers. This form of *demonstration* has long held a noticeable, if somewhat romantic, association with the early grades of the elementary and grammar school. Although occasionally found on the middle school or junior high level, it is in the early grades that an observer will notice the exuberance and sense of life in students who demonstrate, show and tell, what *they* know about a topic. The important message for teachers is that demonstrations enable the student to associate information with a personal memory of accomplishment.

We can easily remember times long ago when we shared our demonstrations with others. We had ownership, as do the students of today, of creating something to share. As we examine our memories of those long-ago successes, we find a common emotion in that experience, the idea of *fun*. Our "show and tells," our sharing with peers and teachers, was fun. Long after most memories of schooling and curriculum content have faded, these *enjoyable experiences* may well become the memories of learning and finding academic success. Unfortunately fun might be the element often missing in the current structure of junior and senior high school learning experiences.

If we as teachers have failed because we have not created and promoted classroom activities that are fun and relevant, then we have made a serious mistake. If our reliance on a monodimensional frame of learning has led us to rule out the "show and tell" or other demonstrations, we have taken a wrong turn and need to right our course. Although the junior and senior high school level programs do not often include the demonstration, it remains in vogue at the highest levels of organized formal education. How many of us have made presentations in graduate classes? In one perspective, a doctoral dissertation is a grand celebration in which one demonstrates what one has discovered, the ultimate "show and tell."

Demonstrations are celebrations of sorts. They celebrate creativity and the process of producing a final product, though, as one graduate teacher constantly reminded Joe, "every draft is actually the penultimate draft" because there is always something, in hindsight, we might have done differently. Therefore we believe that offering students the opportunity to present, to demonstrate, and to defend their knowledge can be one of the most empowering strategies for learning. Again, the teacher is a special person in this process. Teachers are the guides who enable students to achieve a sense of ownership for their exploration and demonstration. Teachers are also the coaches who help students realize the importance of personal accountability in their designs and demonstrations.

AN OVERVIEW OF THE MECHANICS

In offering a demonstration, the presenter needs to answer five basic questions: *who, what, when, where,* and *why*. Taken from another angle, the presenter needs to offer an example of what they learned and the underlying story behind the example.

Topic Selection

Part of the involvement that demonstrations can generate comes from the student-centered nature of these strategies. Students can *select* their topics for demonstration. This selection can be from a teacher-generated list of possible topics or from a student's examination of a unit's contents. We have arranged our student selections both ways. When students make a choice and create their own topics within the framework of a unit outline, they are more vested in the presentation. However, teacher-generated topics are always handy for some students who need support or a bit of direction, especially early in the strategy development.

Length

Demonstrations can be long term, short term, or somewhere in the middle. They can supplement a unit or specific topic or frame the central core of a unit. All of this is up to the teacher to decide. Again, we cannot understate the importance of a teacher as a guide in setting the direction for a class and in shaping an individual student's learning experiences.

Requirements and Accountability

Some voices will always ask about the requirements and accountability of strategies that advocate students having fun. Unfortunately in some classes teachers boxcar fun activities in which the relevance to a unit of study or a common strand tying the activities together was missing or not properly identified. But students are working within a framework that requires them to produce but does not offer, in the short term, the visible and attractive rewards that students see from actual employment. Consequently, fun is a legitimate short-term motivator and activator. However, we have built a number of steps into our activities that ensure accountability and offer evidence that students are learning while having fun. In the following outlines of our strategies, students are expected to submit a bibliography and a fact or information sheet as a part of their presentation. The student-produced documents are collected, itemized, and eventually built into the final product. They are the required substantiation for a cumulative period of research as well as examples of the learning process. This applies to both bibliographic information and "fact" or "informational" sheets.

THE OPENNESS OF THE MODEL

The demonstration strategies that follow enable students to select and design the topic and to choose the method of demonstration. Simply stated, this means that the *understood* expectation is that more than a bibliography or a fact sheet is required.

THE ISSUE OF COOPERATIVE WORK

The act of *demonstrating* something to someone else is a cooperative experience. Explaining to another makes one a peer educator because the presenter shares knowledge gained through research. The strategies we offer under the rubric of the demonstration lead to cooperative teaching experiences in which students educate their peers.

Because these strategies lead to culminating cooperative activities, an additional facet of student collaboration must be built into the presentation. Although the teacher can arrange the size of the groups in which students work, all students are focused on a designated content area. Individual students, pairs of students, or groups of three or more students will be working on specific topics within that content area. Again, we leave the decision of the size and makeup of work units to the classroom teacher, who best knows the diversity and needs of a particular class. Although demonstrations offer golden opportunities for cooperative experiences, we see the process in terms of a class as a cooperative unit. Our individual work aggregates are rarely larger than three students when working on collaborative presentations. Often our students present as individuals or partners yet work within the class-group in preparing what they will present. But these are decisions of the classroom teacher.

THE STRATEGIES: A DESCRIPTION

We have placed our demonstration strategies into eight loose groups. As with the interviews outlined in chapter 3, we believe that flexibility offers freedom for teachers. Our strategies are not rigid and may be modified by teachers to fit the needs of particular classrooms. Always think of these strategies as flexible and open to innovation.

Who Am I's?

We have used this tried and true activity again and again. It is geared toward segments of time in a historical sense. Our students have brought many specific individuals to life in our classrooms, and they have also recreated the lives of common people, portraying average citizens of a particular time. For example, in one class after Julius Caesar told us about himself and his view of life in Rome, he was followed by two slaves from Gaul who offered their views. As our following examples show, "Who Am I's?" require a timed presentation and a follow-up activity for the rest of the class.

" . . . Days"

One of our first attempts at a "day" was called "Mid East Day." It was done with seventh graders who were working in a unit on North Africa and the Middle East. The day was designed to be a time when our students could showcase some aspect of life in the cultural region under study. In addition to the general knowledge explored by the unit, students would have the opportunity to research, explore, and develop a more personal knowledge about a specific aspect of life in that cultural region. In the process of dovetailing the more general unit material with the student's more specific personal research, both students and teachers discovered that the two areas of learning were overwhelmingly interconnected. For example, students could clearly see through their own research how a general topic such as climate directly impacted their specific topics of farming or growth and location of cities.

Our first "Mid East Day" involved 86 seventh graders, who turned the school's cafeteria into a facsimile of a Mid Eastern bazaar. The tables were arranged in rows to replicate narrow streets lined with booths. In each booth a student, in costume with as much material as the student wished, demonstrated, through conversations with visitors, what he or she had learned about the topic, while selling artifacts, food, and other goods. The presentation lasted two hours and included tourists from the student body, the faculty, parents, and the community.

This example, focusing on one topic at one grade level, clearly shows that the demonstration strategy has a variety of applications and can successfully work with any number of students.

"A Taste Of"

What better way to come to understand a culture of today or one from the past than to share in its culinary heritage. Taste of's feature student-prepared foods based on knowledge gained through research. The final product of the research is a buffet style dinner where students share the dishes they created. Before the meal, each student briefly describes the dish, where they located the recipe, and its preparation.

"The Fair"

Like the demonstration of a "day," various opportunities for classroom work are presented by hosting a fair. Fairs can be used either to supplement or to provide structure to a unit. Their scope can include time periods, political units, or cultural groups. They can model any of the multitude of fairs that are held throughout our society and can feature whatever activities fairs popularize. This activity is also flexible in that it can be adjusted to fit specific requirements such as time and space. For example, a fair could highlight a unit on colonial New England as students prepare foods, demonstrate games, and exhibit styles of clothing and manufactured goods of the period.

The Museum and Its Artifacts

Another type of demonstration that can easily fit into a history class or other social studies course exploring a different culture or period is the museum. Using this strategy, students create a museum in which each member of the class displays an artifact from the area under study. The artifacts could range from household utensils and forms of technology to more creative mediums such as masks and ceremonial costumes. In addition, students then describe the creation and uses of the displayed artifact.

Map Making

Maps are an integral part of social studies classes, and some maps should be created by the student. Too often we simply provide maps that need to be labeled, colored in, or traced. Yet map creations should be a measure of knowledge. Students need to be *cartographers*. As such, maps should not be one person's product shared only with a teacher before disappearing forever. Maps should be shown to others. They should be explained, dissected, and displayed. Maps are an effective way of demonstrating what students have learned.

Time Lines

As with maps, time lines represent the stuff of social studies. They show chronologies, perspectives, and themes. Time lines, like maps, can be of any size. They are student created and should be shared, displayed, and explained. We have included some variations on time lines our students have created.

Advertisements

Advertisements are understood and enjoyed by many of us because they are such an ingrained part of our culture. As a result of the students' knowledge of and relationship to advertisements in contemporary society, these demonstrations can be fun to create. The strategy requires students to develop an advertisement that sells a product from the period being studied. Advertisements can be produced using audio tape, video tape, or print and posters. They can focus on a particular article, an idea, a person, or a place. Advertisements are an interesting supplemental demonstration to any unit.

FORMS AND EVALUATION

The forms we used to feature the interview strategies discussed in chapter 3 were designed to be used by a teacher to structure a classroom activity. We created these forms, which describe our sample demonstrations, to focus the activity of the student or a work group of students. In addition, the forms serve as an agreement, a contract of sorts, through which teacher and students list what will constitute a particular demonstration. The forms are geared to an individual student's activity rather than to that of an entire class. When students and teacher complete the form, it serves as an outline for the student as well as an evaluation tool. We have included sample demonstration forms in the Appendix.

Sample
Demonstration
Strategies

Course:	World History/Western Civilization/ European History
Length of Activity:	Two weeks
Grade Level:	9–10
Unit:	Reformation
Topic:	Reasons for Religious Upheaval
Title:	Martin Luther
Description of Activity:	Who Am I?
Overview:	In this activity a student will take on the persona of Martin Luther. The student selects the topic. The student is required to do a five- to seven-minute presentation for the class, describing the life of Luther as Luther would describe it today. Student may use index cards, props, and whatever else is deemed necessary to complete the presentation. The student is also required to distribute to the class one handout (crossword puzzle, word search, etc.) that relates directly to the presentation. The student is also expected to dress in character. Three class days during a two-week period will be devoted to library research. Presentations will take place during the third week. This activity is a supplement to an ongoing unit.
Number of Students:	1 (of a class of 30)
Concepts:	1. The meaning of the Reformation 2. The Christian interpretation of the afterlife 3. The issue of indulgences 4. The reasons for the spread of Protestantism
Factual Information:	Martin Luther, indulgences, protestants, the Pope, Johann Tetzel, Reformation, Lutheranism, ninety-five theses, Peasants' Revolt, Peace of Augsburg
Skills:	1. Library research 2. Organizing a presentation 3. Developing instructional materials 4. Costume design 5. Completing a presentation

Timetable of Activities:

TIME FRAME (BY WEEK/BY DAY)

(Week 1) One class day of library research

(Week 2) Two class days of library research

(Week 3) Presentation scheduled with others from class.

Evaluation: Student self-evaluation of objectives highlighted on this form (see also the Student Evaluation Form in the Appendix). Teacher evaluation of same. Student self-evaluation of presentation, including handout, costume, and presentation. Teacher evaluation of same. Peer evaluation of student presentation. Weekly teacher evaluation of student progress in library research (see Bibliography form in the Appendix).

Corollaries to Murphy's Law: Some students will not want to present. Some students will present for more than 10 minutes, which could extend the lesson indefinitely.

Course:	American Studies
Length of Activity:	Five days
Grade Level:	10
Unit:	Slavery in Pre–Civil War America
Topic:	Horrors and Injustices of Enslaving People
Title:	Great African Americans Speak Out
Description of Activity:	Who Am I?
Overview:	In this activity a student will take on the persona of one of six great African Americans from the period before the Civil War. The students either select the topic or it can be teacher assigned. Each student is required to do a five- to seven-minute presentation for the class describing the life of the historical person as that person would describe it today. Students may use index cards, props, and whatever else is deemed necessary to complete the presentation. The students are also required to distribute to the class one handout (crossword puzzle, word splash, etc.) that relates directly to the presentation. The students are also expected to dress in character. Five class days during a two-week period will be devoted to library research. Presentations will take place during the third week. The activity will begin with each student entering in costume and telling the class about himself or herself. After this opening presentation from each character, the characters will compose a panel. A student moderator will take questions from the audience for each character. These questions will be from the presentation as well as made up before the presentation. This activity is a supplement to an ongoing unit on the events and people of the period before and during the Civil War. At the same time other students may be conducting research on other significant pre-Civil War and Civil War characters (see Corollaries).
Number of Students:	7
List of Roles:	Harriet Tubman, Nat Turner, Dred Scott, Sojourner Truth, Fredrick Douglas, Denmark Vescey, moderator
Concepts:	1. Effects of slavery on a person
	2. Impact of congressional legislation on the life of a slave
	3. Division of a society
	4. Moral issues within society and government
Factual Information:	Dred Scott Decision, Fugitive Slave Law, *Uncle Tom's Cabin,* Kansas-Nebraska Act, raid on Harper's Ferry, John Brown, personal liberty laws, abolitionists, William Lloyd Garrison, The Liberator

Skills: 1. Library research

              2. Organizing a presentation

              3. Developing instructional materials

              4. Costume design

              5. Completing a presentation

Timetable of Activities:

TIME FRAME (BY WEEK/BY DAY)

(Week 1) Two class days of library research

(Week 2) Two class days of writing scripts, rehearsing

(Week 3) Presentation scheduled with others from class

Evaluation: Student self-evaluation of objectives highlighted on this form (See also Student Evaluation Form in the Appendix). Teacher evaluation of same. Student self-evaluation of presentation including handout and costume. Teacher evaluation of same. Peer evaluation of student presentation. Weekly teacher evaluation of student progress in library research (see Bibliography form in the Appendix).

Corollaries to Murphy's Law: Some students will not want to present. Some students will present for more than 10 minutes, which could extend the lesson indefinitely. This strategy also works very well as part of a unit in which other students are completing research on other historical figures. When Kerry does this activity he also has a group of students who do Civil War generals, both Union and Confederate, including, among others, Robert E. Lee, James Longstreet, Nathan Bedford Forest, George Meade, Ulysses S. Grant, and Joshua Chamberlain. Another group works on Jefferson Davis, Abraham Lincoln, John Brown, and John Wilkes Booth, among others. Consequently, all class members are involved, and this is a thorough way of understanding the impact people have on history.

Course:	American Studies
Length of Activity:	Six days
Grade Level:	10
Unit:	Civil War
Topic:	Events That Changed History
Title:	The Battle of Gettysburg
Description of Activity:	Blends elements of Who Am I?, Map Making, Museum, and Time Lines
Overview:	Students at this grade level are asked to take part in recreating the Battle of Gettysburg. The battle recreation will take place in the classroom, a private but larger area of the school, or if the school is fortunate to have them, on spacious grounds with rolling hills (even football fields, softball/baseball outfields, or soccer fields work well). Students are assigned to one of three groups: the Union army, the Confederate army, and the citizenry of Gettysburg. Research will take place for five days of class time. Research should include making maps showing the locations of the major forces for each army, the landmarks in the town and on the battlefield, and the changes that occur each day. Students should consider factors such as size of each army, breakdown of army, key leaders, and important strategies, the causes and effects of the battle, and the effects of the battle on people and the town. On the sixth day, students will reenact major movements of the battle, culminating with Pickett's charge. Students are encouraged to come dressed in appropriate clothing. The "Battle" will take place the following week on a designated battlefield. Students will be required to complete a battlefield map, an outline of their involvement, a narrative response written after the event highlighting key events and decisions, and a bibliography. This demonstration is meant to complement a unit on the Civil War. Students engage in living the part for the presentation.
Number of Students:	Full class
Concepts:	1. Historical chance
	2. Decision making of leaders
	3. Battlefield strategies
	4. Effects of war on armies, nations
	5. Human toll in battle
	6. Physical and spatial arrangements

Factual Information: July 1, 2, 3, 1863, Robert E. Lee, James Longstreet, George Pickett, George Meade, Joshua Chamberlain, Daniel Sickles, Joshua Reynolds, John Buford, Little Round Top, the Wheatfield, Devil's Den, artillery, casualties, Army of the Potomac, Army of Northern Virginia, other facts students may uncover in their research and deem important to the presentation.

Skills:
1. Library research
2. Organizing a presentation
3. Developing instructional materials
4. Costume design
5. Completing a presentation
6. Map making
7. Cooperative effort
8. Following directions

Timetable of Activities:

TIME FRAME (BY DAY)

(Day 1) Assign roles, construct battlefield maps

(Day 2) Continuing research: causes of battle

(Day 3) Continuing research: makeup of army, leaders

(Day 4) Continuing research: major decisions

(Day 5) Continuing research: effects of the battle

(Day 6) The battle

Evaluation: Student self-evaluation of objectives highlighted on this form (see also Student Evaluation Form in the Appendix). Teacher evaluation of same. Student self-evaluation of presentation, including handout, costume, and presentation. Teacher evaluation of same. Peer evaluation of student presentation. Daily teacher evaluation of students' progress in library research (see Bibliography form in the Appendix).

Corollaries to Murphy's Law: Two factors that can affect the staging of the battle are time, meaning class period length, and the weather if you decide to do the reconstruction outside. Another drawback is student absenteeism on the final day. A positive side to this activity is the involvement factor as opposed to the motivation issue. As students become involved in the activity, a sense of ownership builds that increases their desire to see an activity through to its conclusion even if they are not highly motivated by the subject matter.

Course: Western Civilization

Length of Activity: Two weeks

Grade Level: 9–10

Unit: Prehistoric Times

Topic: Neanderthals and Cro-Magnons

Title: Neanderthals and Cro-Magnons Compare Themselves with Homo Sapiens of Today

Description of Activity: Who Am I?

Overview: In this activity two students will take on the personae of a Neanderthal and a Cro-Magnon. The pair of students selected the topic from the unit outline. Each student is required to do a five- to seven-minute presentation for the class describing the life of Cro-Magnons and Neanderthals and compare it with the life of Homo sapiens today. Students may use index cards, props, and whatever else is deemed necessary to complete the presentation. The students are also each required to distribute to the class one handout (crossword puzzle, word search, etc.) that relates directly to the presentation. The students are also expected to dress in character. Three class days during a two-week period will be devoted to library research. Presentations will take place during the third week. This activity is a supplement to an ongoing unit.

Number of Students: 2 (of a class of 20)

Concepts:
1. What creates a civilization?
2. The importance of government
3. Technology
4. Division of labor
5. Relationship of a written language to a society
6. What does it mean to have a "culture?"

Factual Information: Domesticate, culture, pictographs, Neanderthals, Cro-Magnon, prehistoric, B.C., A.D., Homo sapiens, New Stone Age, Old Stone Age

Skills:
1. Library research
2. Organizing a presentation
3. Developing instructional materials
4. Costume design
5. Completing a presentation

Timetable of Activities:

TIME FRAME (BY WEEK/BY DAY)

(Week 1) One class day of library research

(Week 2) Two class days of library research

(Week 3) Presentation scheduled with others from class

Evaluation: Student self-evaluation of objectives highlighted on this form (see also Student Evaluation Form in the Appendix). Teacher evaluation of same. Student self-evaluation of presentation, including handout, costume, and presentation. Teacher evaluation of same. Peer evaluation of student presentation. Weekly teacher evaluation of student progress in library research (see Bibliography form in the Appendix).

Corollaries to Murphy's Law: Students have had to be reminded by Joe Nowicki to create a costume that does not violate current codes and covers vital parts.

Course:	World Geography
Length of Activity:	Seven to nine weeks
Grade Level:	7–8
Unit:	The Middle East
Topic:	Student-Generated Issue Regarding the Middle East and North Africa
Title:	Middle East Day
Description of Activity:	" . . . Day"

Overview: Middle East Day brings together an entire class or grade and engages them in a common presentation composed of many individual presentations. The activity begins with students selecting topics concerning aspects of life and history from this culture region of the world. For example, students have chosen to do their presentations on a particular country, a religion, a group of people (for example, bedouins), a language, ancient history in the region (Egypt, Mesopotamia, Sumer, among others), the music of the region, the art of the region, the resources of the region, the natural features of the region (Nile River, Red Sea, Dead Sea), particular historical characters, and many other subjects. Students prepare for their presentation by doing their research during time allotted from class and on their own. They must follow a weekly sheet of "resource checks" as they build bibliographies (see form in the Appendix).

As "Mid East Day" nears, students develop an outline of what their presentation will entail. Usually this outline includes

1. Their costume

2. A description of the factual material they will present and how they will present it (maps, displays, fact sheets, graphs).

3. A sample of the "hands-on" material they will display or sell (food, artifacts such as a sarcophagus, water they claim comes from the Nile, sand from the Sahara . . . these are but a few of the hundreds of topics and items used as props for presentations during the past five years).

4. A description of a demonstration they are designing for the day of something that they have become "an expert at" (playing live music, teaching a visitor how to write in hieroglyphics, demonstrating how an oil well works with a model, explaining why a camel is suited for desert travel or why the Sahara is expanding, again among many other possible demonstrations).

On "Mid East Day" students are given time to prepare their demonstrations and a large area (in this case the cafeteria of the school) is organized into a series of rows. Students set up booths along the rows for their demonstrations. After a certain time the rest of the student body, parents, and members of the local communities are admitted to the area, which now

111

replicates a bazaar. The day is videotaped and used to both evaluate the presentations and display the activities to the next year's class.

Number of Students: 97 (last year)

Concepts:
1. Knowledge of a different culture region of the world
2. The idea of interdependence in a world community and between people and their environment
3. A recognition of the importance of diversity in our society

Factual Information: The information contained within the outline of the unit and whatever students discover through their own research and demonstrate to others

Skills:
1. Researching
2. Organization
3. Presentation
4. Teaching

Timetable of Activities:

TIME FRAME (BY WEEK/BY DAY)

(Week 1) Students select topic and begin outline of research

(Week 2) One class day allocated for library research

(Week 3) One class day allocated for library research

(Week 4) One class day allocated for library research, students complete bibliography form check 1

(Week 5) One class day allocated for library research, students complete outline 1

(Week 6) One class day allocated for library research, students complete bibliography form check 2

(Week 7) One class day allocated for library research

(Week 8) One class day allocated for project final preparation; final outlines and bibliography sheets due

(Week 9) Mid East Day

Evaluation: Teacher evaluation of bibliography sheets and progress, student outlines, and final demonstration. Outside evaluators (other faculty members) are asked to evaluate specific student presentations using a standardized evaluation sheet. Students evaluate peer presentations. Students complete a self-evaluation as a narrative writing exercise after the completion of Mid East Day.

Corollaries to Murphy's Law: The Gulf War began one Mid East Day, prompting some anxiety about the reactions from the older members of the student body. There were no negative ones. Actually, one can only imagine how much can go wrong given so many presentations, though for most students the day has produced some grand memories.

Course:	American History
Length of Activity:	Two weeks
Grade Level:	11–12
Unit:	The Revolution
Topic:	Colonial Life
Title:	Thirteen Colonies Day
Description of Activity:	". . . Day"
Overview:	Students at this grade level are asked to take part in recreating a day in the pre-Revolutionary colonies. The day will take place in the classroom or in a private but larger area of the school. Each student is asked to prepare something for the day that reflects a knowledge of colonial life. Students are encouraged to come dressed in appropriate clothing. Research will take place for three days of class time. The "Day" will take place the following week. Students will be required to complete a final outline of their presentation, a narrative response written after the event, and a bibliography. This demonstration is meant to complement a unit on the Revolution. Students engage in living the part for the presentation.
Number of Students:	25–30
Concepts:	1. The characteristics of colonial life before the Revolution as opposed to life after the Revolution
	2. An understanding of why some colonists supported the Revolution and why some did not
Factual Information:	Individual- and group-generated knowledge about colonial life and the Revolution
Skills:	1. Researching
	2. Presentation
Timetable of Activities:	

TIME FRAME (BY WEEK/BY DAY)

(Week 1) Researching for three days during class time

(Week 2) Presentation of the "day." Evaluation of bibliography, outline, and presentation. Student narrative

Evaluation:	Teacher evaluation of student progress. Teacher evaluation of student presentations. Student self- and peer evaluation.

Corollaries to
Murphy's Law: This activity has been a lot of fun, though evaluation can be a problem because students are celebrating the day and living presentations rather than actually doing a formal presentation.

Course:	Civics/American Government
Length of Activity:	Three weeks
Grade Level:	8
Unit:	Town Government
Topic:	Town Life and Interdependence
Title:	Town Fair
Description of Activity:	A Fair

Overview: Students research the diversity and interdependence their town has to offer, and they present one aspect they have discovered. This strategy is meant to provide background for an existing unit on town government. Research is done as homework assignments. Students are required to turn in an outline of their research along with their presentations. Presentations are to be made within the small group of the classroom. One day, the week before the Fair, students will describe their outline and what they wish to share.

Number of Students: 20–25

Concepts:
1. The interdependence of town or city life
2. The unique character of town or city life

Factual Information: Information unique to the specific town or city, supplied on outline

Skills:
1. Researching
2. Organization
3. Presentation

Timetable of Activities:

TIME FRAME (BY WEEK/BY DAY)

(Week 1) Research begins

(Week 2) Research continues, outlines due

(Week 3) Presentation due during one class meeting

Evaluation: Teacher evaluation of student outline and presentation, student evaluation of peer presentations, student self-evaluation

Corollaries to Murphy's Law: Students can be overwhelmed by the amount of material about their town.

Course:	Civics/American Government
Length of Activity:	3–6 weeks
Grade Level:	8
Unit:	Town Government
Topic:	Town Life and Interdependence
Title:	Town Fair
Description of Activity:	A Fair

Overview: Students research the diversity and interdependence another town has to offer and present one aspect that they have discovered. They gain their information through a three-week teacher-arranged letter exchange with a similar class in another town. This strategy is meant to provide background for an existing unit on town government. Research is done through letter writing and through whatever the class can develop as sources of shared information. Students are required to turn in an outline of their research along with thier presentations. Presentations are to be made within the small group of the classroom and each concern one topic of interest in another town. One day, the week before the Fair, students will describe their outlines and the topics they wish to share.

Number of Students: 20–25

Concepts:
1. The interdependence of town or city life
2. The unique character of town or city life

Factual Information: Information unique to the specific town or city, supplied on outline

Skills:
1. Researching
2. Organization
3. Letter writing
4. Interpretation of another's insights
5. Presentation of analysis

Timetable of Activities:

TIME FRAME (BY WEEK/BY DAY)

(Week 1) Letter writing begins

(Week 2) Additional research continues

(Week 4) Return letters arrive

(Week 5) Organization of presentation during one class day

(Week 6) Presentation day, student outlines due

Evaluation: Teacher evaluation of student outline and presentation, student evaluation of peer presentations, student self-evaluation

Corollaries to
Murphy's Law: The cooperating teacher makes sure students respond with letters that supply enough information about their town.

Course:	Eastern Studies
Length of Activity:	Two days
Grade Level:	11–12
Unit:	China
Topic:	Culture and Daily Life
Title:	A Taste of Shanghai
Description of Activity:	A Taste of . . .
Overview:	Students research the food of Shanghai as part of their study of that part of China. Their research leads them to prepare a dish for class in creating a buffet for the entire class. All students are expected to produce an item. They are also required to write a narrative of how they prepared the recipe.
Number of Students:	25–30
Concepts:	1. Relationship of food and environment to Chinese life 2. Interdependence of society with resources and economy
Factual Information:	Narrative describing student's contribution and why that contribution is reflective of Shanghai
Skills:	1. Researching for recipe 2. Cooking the contribution to the buffet
Timetable of Activities:	

TIME FRAME (BY WEEK/BY DAY)

(Day 1)   Class time dedicated to researching contribution

(Day 2)   Presentation of preprepared meal

Evaluation:	Teacher evaluation of narrative and of student efforts, student self-evaluation, peer evaluation
Corollaries to Murphy's Law:	Anyone attempting this type of presentation needs to ensure a place for food storage and supply utensils. It makes sense to prepare a menu a day ahead of time.

Course:	Ancient History
Length of Activity:	Two days
Grade Level:	9–10
Unit:	Greece
Topic:	Culture and Daily Life
Title:	A Taste of Greece
Description of Activity:	A Taste of . . .
Overview:	Students research the food of modern and ancient Greece as a part of their study of the ancient world. Their research leads them to prepare a dish for class in creating a buffet for the entire class. All students are expected to produce an item. They are also required to write a narrative of how they arrived at their recipe.
Number of Students:	25–30
Concepts:	1. Relationship of food and environment to Greek life 2. Interdependence of society with resources and economy
Factual Information:	Narrative describing student's contribution and why that contribution is reflective of Greece
Skills:	Researching for recipe, cooking the contribution to the buffet
Timetable of Activities:	**TIME FRAME (BY WEEK/BY DAY)** (Day 1) Class time dedicated to researching contribution (Day 2) Presentation of preprepared meal
Evaluation:	Teacher evaluation of narrative and of student efforts, student self-evaluation, peer evaluation
Corollaries to Murphy's Law:	Anyone attempting this type of presentation needs to ensure a place for food storage and supply utensils. It makes sense to prepare a menu a day ahead of time. Teacher needs to provide resources for students to use before students need them.

Course:	World History/Western Civilization
Length of Activity:	Two weeks
Grade Level:	9–10
Unit:	French Revolution
Topic:	Reign of Terror
Title:	Guillotine
Description of Activity:	Museum

Overview: The class is engaged in developing artifacts they will present in a "Museum" format for one day. This activity is part of a larger unit. It includes two days of class time dedicated to library research and one day, at the end of the second week, which will be dedicated for the "Museum." This activity description reflects the efforts of two of the students in the class in designing their "artifact."

Two students have chosen to build a "guillotine." It is to meet exact specifications, and the students are required to submit plans for building it as well as a two-page written narrative describing the history and uses of the guillotine. They are also required to hand in a bibliography sheet at the end of the activity.

Number of Students: 2 (from a class of 24)

Concepts:
1. Capital punishment in society
2. The effects of the French Revolution on daily life in France
3. How terror can be used as a tool for social control

Factual Information: Reign of Terror, Robespierre, Danton, Marat, Louis XVI, Marie Antoinette, guillotine

Skills: Research and application of research to building an artifact

Timetable of Activities:

TIME FRAME (BY WEEK/BY DAY)

(Week 1) One day dedicated to library research

(Week 2) One day dedicated to library research, one day for presentation

Evaluation: Teacher evaluation of student presentation, student self- and peer evaluation written as narrative, student submission of bibliography and narrative explanation

Corollaries to
Murphy's Law: With this particular artifact we had to be extra careful to avoid injuries, and Joe Nowicki needed a very secure place to store it.

Course:	American History
Length of Activity:	Two weeks
Grade Level:	10–11
Unit:	1930s
Topic:	(Student Choice) Transportation
Title:	Pan American Clippers
Description of Activity:	Museum
Overview:	The class is engaged in developing artifacts they will present in a "Museum" format for one day. This activity is part of a larger unit. It includes two days of class time dedicated to library research and one day, at the end of the second week, which will be dedicated to the "Museum." This activity description reflects the efforts of one student in the class opting to design his own "artifact."
	This student has decided to build a model of a "Pan American Clipper." It is to meet exact specifications and the student is required to submit plans for building it as well as a two-page written narrative describing the history of the Clippers. He is also required to hand in a bibliography sheet at the end of the activity.
Number of Students:	1 (from a class of 27)
Concepts:	1. Impact of "global" forms of transportation on the world
	2. Advancements in technology make travel easier
Factual Information:	(Student generates information specific to artifact topic)
Skills:	Research and application of research to building an artifact
Timetable of Activities:	

TIME FRAME (BY WEEK/BY DAY)

(Week 1) One day dedicated to library research

(Week 2) One day dedicated to library research, one day for presentation

Evaluation:	Teacher evaluation of student presentation, student self- and peer evaluation written as narrative, student submission of bibliography and narrative explanation

**Corollaries to
Murphy's Law:** Students might decide on topics that are much larger and require a longer time than is expected.

Course:	World History
Length of Activity:	Five days
Grade Level:	9
Unit:	The Birth of Civilization
Topic:	Growth of Village Life; 8000 to 3000 B.C.
Title:	My Life as an Early Hunter/Gatherer/Farmer
Description of Activity:	Museum

Overview: This activity is based on the complete unit of the study of early humans. One day of class time will be dedicated to library research and preparation. The rest of the work is completed for homework. Another class day is dedicated to the museum activity. One half of the class assume roles of hunters and gatherers, the other half of the class are farmers. Each student has a space in the classroom to set up an artifact or demonstration representing the society or culture. Through the artifacts, exhibitions, and demonstrations, students will portray scenes from the life of early humans.

Number of Students: In a class of twenty, ten will represent the hunters/gatherers, ten will portray the farmers.

Concepts:
1. Domestication
2. Development of agriculture
3. Division of labor
4. Growth of technology

Factual Information: Prehistory, Stone Age, New Stone Age, artifact, culture, fossil, carbon 14 dating, nomad, Ice Age, glacier, migrate, hunting, gathering, technology, artisans, excavate

Skills:
1. Research skills
2. Ability to personalize and subjectify important concepts of history
3. Assuming historical persona
4. Oral speaking skills

Timetable of Activities:

TIME FRAME (BY WEEK/BY DAY)

(Day 1)   Explain and assign

(Day 2)   Full period will be dedicated to library research

(Day 3) Students will continue research for homework and will submit a check sheet of progress explaining the exhibit, artifact, and/or demonstration.

(Day 4) Students will continue research for homework

(Day 5) Presentations

Evaluation:
1. The hunters/gathers will evaluate the life of the farmers, and the farmers will evaluate the hunters/gatherers. Each student will submit a one-page narrative of their findings.

2. Students will complete the form identifying the skills, factual knowledge, and concepts that they will learn through the experience. This form will be the basis of evaluation. How well did the students do what they said they were going to do?

3. Judge the seriousness of the presentation, the depth of research evident in the characterization, the thoroughness and creativity of the presentation.

Corollaries to Murphy's Law: Students must be held to a time limit or the program can go on far too long. Because this activity generally occurs early in the year, students should work in pairs or groups of three. Teachers must also monitor the competition that sometimes springs up between the two cultures.

Course:	World History
Length of Activity:	Three days
Grade Level:	9
Unit:	Ancient Civilizations
Topic:	Egypt
Title:	My Life as a . . .
Description of Activity:	Who Am I?
Overview:	As we concentrate on the growth of civilization and culture, it is important to examine an early civilization in greater depth to understand what elements, activities, and classes of people composed the culture. Consequently a "Who Am I" of the Egyptian culture/civilization is to continue the process of recognizing change, growth, and the development of society. The questions of how civilization and culture evolve are continually looked at as important to examining our own culture and civilization. Students will have five minutes for their characters. Students must use props, dress, and various devices to explore their characters.
Number of Students:	20 students; each student will perform as a character, and the other class members serve as audience and questioners.
Concepts:	1. Religion and its importance in Egypt
	2. Role of pharaohs, use of power
	3. Structure of Egyptian society
	4. Civilization
	5. Culture
Factual Information:	Dynasty, pharaoh, hieroglyphics, papyrus, Rosetta Stone, surplus, tribute, Ramses II, Tutankhamen, Cleopatra, Menes, pyramids, Osiris, Isis, Nile, mummification, Book of the Dead, Giza, Middle Kingdom, New Kingdom
Skills:	1. Research skills
	2. Assuming historical persona
	3. Oral speaking skills
	4. Ability to subjectify important historical data

Timetable of Activities:

TIME FRAME (BY WEEK/BY DAY)

(Day 1)   Explain and define

(Day 2)   Library research

(Day 3)   Presentation

Corollaries to Murphy's Law: Presentations must stay within the time limit. Also there is some resistance earlier in the year on the part of students. As the activity continued, this generally vanished.

Course:	World History
Length of Activity:	Two days
Grade Level:	9
Unit:	The Middle Ages
Topic:	Daily Life in Middle Ages
Title:	A Taste of a Medieval Banquet
Description of Activity:	A Taste of . . .

Overview: For students to gain understanding of history, it is important to continually personalize in as many ways as possible. One way to do this is to develop situations in which the students create a daily event in a historical period, which allows students to make comparisons to their own life and time. Food and eating customs and habits are an excellent, high-interest way of achieving this goal. Working in pairs, students will find recipes from the medieval period and prepare a dish. The class will arrange the room into the design of a medieval banquet hall.

Number of Students: 20. This works well with any number.

Concepts:
1. Daily life
2. Roles and duties in Middle Ages
3. Role of family unit

Factual Information: Middle Ages, fief, vassal, knight, chivalry, manor, manorial system, serf, clergy, spread of Germanic customs

Skills:
1. Making decisions
2. Interpreting and personalizing history
3. Organization
4. Oral speaking

Timetable of Activities:

TIME FRAME (BY WEEK/BY DAY)

(Day 1) Explain and assign roles

(Day 2) Research

(Day 3) Presentation and eating

Evaluation: Each student/pair will explain to the class and submit a one-page paper delineating where they found their recipe, any problems in finding the ingredients for the dish, what they think about the dish, and what they can determine about the life in the Middle Ages from this activity.

Corollaries to
Murphy's Law: Time is a big issue here. For this to be effective, it needs about one hour. Additionally, all phases of the presentation and cleanup must be clearly outlined for the class. Every student must have a role, especially in cleanup. You also need a cooperative cafeteria staff or home economics department for the use of refrigerators or stoves.

Course:	World History
Length of Activity:	Two days
Grade Level:	9
Unit:	World War I
Topic:	Daily Life in Paris
Title:	A Visit to a Parisian Sidewalk Cafe
Description of Activity:	A Taste of . . .

Overview: For students to gain an understanding of history, it is important to continually personalize the ideas in as many ways as possible. One way to achieve this is by developing situations in which the students create a daily event in a historical period which allows students to make comparisons with their own lives and with the historical period. Food and eating customs and habits are an excellent, high-interest way of achieving this goal. Working in pairs, students will find French recipes popular in the time of World War I and prepare the dishes. The class will arrange the room in the design of a Parisian sidewalk cafe to serve the meal.

Number of Students: 20. This works well with any number.

Concepts:
1. Daily life
2. Roles, duties, and attitudes in prewar France
3. Militarism, imperialism, nationalism

Factual Information: Whatever information the students uncover in their research and share with the class

Skills:
1. Making decisions
2. Interpreting and personalizing history
3. Organization
4. Oral speaking

Timetable of Activities:

TIME FRAME (BY WEEK/BY DAY)

(Day 1)   Explain and assign roles

(Day 2)   Research

(Day 3)   Presentation and eating

135

Evaluation: Each student/pair will explain to the class and submit a one-page report delineating where they found their recipe, any problems in obtaining the ingredients for the dish, what they think about the dish, and what they can determine about the life in pre–World War I France from this activity.

Corollaries to Murphy's Law: Time is a big issue here. For this to be effective, it needs about one hour. Additionally, all phases of the presentation and cleanup must be clearly outlined for the class. Every student must have a role, especially in cleanup. You also need a cooperative cafeteria staff or home economics department for the use of refrigerators or stoves. Possibly consider hiding some antacid tablets in your top drawer for later in the day.

Course:	World History
Length of Activity:	One week
Grade Level:	9
Unit:	The Middle Ages
Topic:	Development of Technology
Title:	The Medieval Museum
Description of Activity:	Museum

Overview: Throughout the study of the growth of culture and civilization, students constantly look at various forms of technology that often drove the changes of a culture. Because many implements of various early cultures are obsolete, it is difficult to examine the utensils. But through this exercise, students recreate models of many early technological advancements. Working in pairs, students research, design, draw up plans for, and build the artifact. For the exhibition, students prepare a museum card to explain the artifact's importance, use, and impact on the culture. On the day of the presentation the room will be arranged in a museum exhibit format. Students circulate in the room to examine the exhibits. This will be followed by a hands-on explanation of each exhibit by the designers.

Number of Students: 20

Concepts:
1. Development, importance, and impact of technology
2. Formation and power of guilds

Factual Information: Guilds, journeyman, masterpiece, apprentice, Gothic architecture, universitas, Summa Theologica, and whatever other information the students discover in their research and share with the class

Skills:
1. Research skills
2. Cooperative interdependence
3. Oral presentation skills
4. Organization

Timetable of Activities:

TIME FRAME (BY WEEK/BY DAY)

(Day 1)   Explain and allow time for preliminary research; assign partners and projects

(Day 2)   Library research

(Day 3)		Students work on projects at home
(Day 4)		Students continue to work on projects at home
(Day 5)		Students present and set up the museum

Evaluation: Students will be judged primarily on the merits of their project. However, special emphasis will be given to effort, quality of the finished product, seriousness of approach, depth of research, creativity, and the overall effect in the exhibit

Corollaries to Murphy's Law: Time is a major problem. Students have to do the work at home. Some students may not have the materials or the transportation to get to each other's homes to work together. We have also found it very beneficial to have a weekend included in the time period.

Course:	World History
Length of Activity:	One week
Grade Level:	9
Unit:	Ancient Civilizations
Topic:	Development of Technology
Title:	The Ancient History Museum
Description of Activity:	Museum

Overview: Throughout the study of the growth of culture and civilization, students look at various forms of technology that often drove the changes of a culture. Because many implements of various early cultures are obsolete, it is difficult to examine the utensils. But through this exercise, students recreate models of many early technological advancements. Working in pairs, students research, design, draw plans for, and build the artifact. For the exhibition, students prepare a museum card to explain the artifact's importance, use, and impact on the culture. On the day of the presentation, the room will be arranged in a museum exhibit format. Students circulate in the room to examine the exhibits. This will be followed by a hands-on explanation of each exhibit by the designers.

Number of Students: 20

Concepts:
1. Development, importance, and impact of technology
2. Examples of early technology that changed the civilization
3. Technological changes were often solutions to problems that confronted humans

Factual Information: Pyramids, hieroglyphics, archeology, mummification, cuneiform, fertile crescent, flooding of Nile, Bronze Age, Stone Age, Copper Age, permanent housing, pottery, farm implements, irrigation, systems of writing, the early alphabets, and any other information students may uncover in their research

Skills:
1. Research skills
2. Cooperative interdependence
3. Oral presentation skills
4. Organization

Timetable of Activities:

TIME FRAME (BY WEEK/BY DAY)

(Day 1)   Explain and allow time for preliminary research

(Day 2)   Students select partners and projects

(Day 3)   Students work on projects at home

(Day 4)   Students continue to work on projects at home

(Day 5)   Students present and set up the museum

Evaluation: Students will be judged primarily on the merits of their project. However, special emphasis will be given to effort, quality of the finished product, seriousness of approach, depth of research, creativity, and the overall effect in the exhibit.

Corollaries to Murphy's Law: Time is a major problem. Students have to do the work at home. Some students may not have the materials or the transportation to get to each other's homes to work together. It is also very helpful to students to include a weekend as part of the time frame for this assignment.

Course:	World History
Length of Activity:	Two days
Grade Level:	9
Unit:	World War I
Topic:	Changes in World Geography
Title:	Map Making: Europe Before and After World War I
Description of Activity:	Map
Overview:	As political boundaries change, history changes. Students need to work with this information by creating maps that allow them to physically experience nations and boundaries. Working in pairs, students first create a map of Europe showing the political divisions and national boundaries in the late 1800s. After the study of World War I, students construct a second map showing the changes in national boundaries. Both maps are constructed on large paper; 2- by 3-foot sheets allow students the space to effectively draw the maps. After completing the postwar maps, students will post both for comparison.
Number of Students:	20

Concepts:
1. Geographic boundaries
2. Political boundaries
3. Nationalism
4. Imperialism

Factual Information: All information that students discover in the researching for the maps

Skills:
1. Map-making skills
2. Research

Timetable of Activities:

TIME FRAME (BY WEEK/BY DAY)

(Day 1) Explain, assign, and begin work

(Day 2) Continue map making

(Day 3) Finish and post

(Day 4) Explain and discuss

Evaluation: Finished maps will be graded with an emphasis on accuracy, effort, appearance, cooperation, seriousness of effort, and neatness of final product. Additionally, students complete a one-page narrative explaining the importance of their findings.

Corollaries to Murphy's Law: Because the work is completed in class, absenteeism is a problem. Students need to be reminded that they should be in class and that is part of the grade. Effective grading is very important in any of these exercises because they require a high degree of cooperative interdependence.

Course:	American Studies
Length of Activity:	Eleven days
Grade Level:	10
Unit:	Colonial America
Topic:	Development of the Colonies
Title:	Fair Day
Description of Activity:	Fair Day
Overview:	This activity serves as a supplement to the main unit on Colonial America and focuses students on the differences that occurred in the developing colonies. Through this activity students will see the colonies develop in two ways. First they will get a feel for the colony as a distinct and, at times, almost separate entity from other colonies. Secondly, through the fair they will have the opportunity to readily compare and contrast the colonies. This foundation enables students to have a stronger sense of colony/ country as the unit proceeds. Working in groups of two or three, depending on class size, students select a specific colony and prepare a full presentation of the economics, produce, government, recreation, and so on, of this particular area. Props, dress, and visuals are very important in this activity. For the fair, students arrange the classroom into 13 booths, each representing a colony.

Number of Students: 20

Concepts:

1. Growth of colonies
2. Regional differences
3. English/European influences
4. Rise of social divisions
5. Influence of changing technology
6. Growth and variety of cultures

Factual Information: Will be determined by the research specific to each colony

Skills:

1. Research skills
2. Cooperative effort
3. Integration of artifacts and ideas
4. Oral presentation skills
5. Creativity

Timetable of Activities:

TIME FRAME (BY WEEK/BY DAY)

(Week 1) Teacher outlines the assignment and students select the colony. Two class periods are dedicated to library research.

(Week 2) One class period is dedicated to library research. Students submit a checklist outlining progress; bibliography sheet is included in this.

(Week 3) Hold the fair.

Evaluation: The final grade will be the presentation at the fair. Emphasis in the grading will be on the amount of research, the seriousness of the display, effort, the cooperative work, the scope of the information presented for the colony, and the creativity in presenting the information through dress, props, displays, and written materials. Students will complete a one-page narrative explaining what they learned. It is also quite helpful to videotape the presentations to assist in evaluation and student self-critiquing.

Corollaries to Murphy's Law: Because a large amount of the project is completed outside of class, you lose a certain degree of control as to what is being done. However, one way to remedy this is to have a few minutes of each period set aside for quick reports, questions, and problems. Depending on length of periods, the fair might need two periods. One method of dealing with this is to do the northern colonies on the first day, and the southern on the second. Then not all students have to prepare and dress, without the disappointment of not having time to present.

Course:	World History
Length of Activity:	Two weeks
Grade Level:	9
Unit:	Ancient Civilizations
Topic:	Development of Civilizations
Title:	Time Capsule Fair Day: Egypt
Description of Activity:	Fair

Overview: Because this activity is an excellent summarizer of the study of early civilizations, it should be timed to coincide with the completion of the unit. It is supplemental to the unit, although it could be designed to function as the unit. Again this decision is best left to the teacher. Through this activity students see the ancient world as a real place where people lived, worked, and recreated. First, they will see each civilization as distinct and separate from other civilizations. Second, through the fair they can compare and contrast the civilizations. This foundation will enable students to have a stronger sense of civilization and the elements of culture as the course proceeds. Working in groups of two or three, depending on class size, students select a specific civilization to prepare a complete presentation of the economics, produce, government, recreation, and technology of this particular area. Props, dress, and visuals are very important in this activity. On the day of the fair, the students will arrange the classroom into centers, with each representing a civilization.

Number of Students: 20

Concepts:
1. Use of artifacts in recreating a culture
2. Regional differences
3. Division of labor
4. Rise of social divisions
5. Influence of changing technology
6. Growth and variety of cultures
7. Growth and development of language
8. Influence of geography on cultural development
9. Reasons for development of government

Factual Information: Determined by the information the students use for their presentations

Skills:　1.　Research skills

2. Cooperative effort

3. Integration of artifacts and ideas

4. Oral presentation skills

5. Creativity

Timetable of Activities:

TIME FRAME (BY WEEK/BY DAY)

(Week 1) Teacher explains assignment and selection of civilization and two classes are dedicated to library research

(Week 2) One class is dedicated to library research, summary and bibliography check list are due.

(Week 3) Hold the fair.

Evaluation: The final grade will be the presentation at the fair. Emphasis in the grading will be on the amount of research, the seriousness of the display, the effort, cooperative attitude, the scope of the information presented for the colony, and the creativity in presenting the information through dress, props, displays, and written materials. Students will complete a fact and information sheet as well as a one-page narrative of what they learned. Videotaping is helpful for evaluation and student self-critiquing.

Corollaries to Murphy's Law: Because a large amount of the project is completed outside of class, you lose a certain degree of control as to what is being done. However, one way to remedy this is to have a few minutes of each period set aside for quick reports, questions, and problems. Again the presentation may last longer than the standard period. Therefore it is advisable to break down the presentations to cover two days. Also, research is more available and complete on some civilizations. Consequently, the teacher needs to guide students to areas that are more easily accessible; otherwise frustration can seriously hinder the progress of a group.

Course:	World History
Length of Activity:	Two days
Grade Level:	9
Unit:	The Middle Ages
Topic:	Understanding Time Limits
Title:	Time Lines
Description of Activity:	Time Line
Overview:	Students will work on completing a time line between 400 A.D. and 1000 A.D. They are to look at issues in world history that had a significant impact on the developing world. The students need not limit themselves to written notations but may also use visuals and pictorials to represent key dates and events. Students use 2- by 3-foot sheets of display paper for the time lines; the teacher will supply various colored markers and materials. The final products are posted in the classroom for discussion and comparison.
Number of Students:	20
Concepts:	1. Cause and effect
	2. Relationships between parallel events in various cultures
	3. Comparing and contrasting
Factual Information:	All factual material is unearthed by the students and placed on the time line.
Skills:	1. Research
	2. Critical thinking skills
	3. Decision making
	4. Oral presentation
Timetable of Activities:	

TIME FRAME (BY WEEK/BY DAY)

(Day 1)   Explain and assign

(Day 2)   Complete project and post

Evaluation: The finished product will be evaluated with an emphasis on neatness, quality of product, significant number of events, and historical accuracy.

Corollaries to Murphy's Law: The work is cooperatively completed in the class; students must be in class.

Course: Geography

Length of Activity: One week

Grade Level: 7–8

Unit: Understanding Maps (first activity in this unit)

Topic: Creating Maps

Title: Mapping Your Way Home

Description of Activity: Map Making

Overview: Maps give people a sense of place and a perspective of where they are in relation to the rest of their environment. In this activity students draw a map from the classroom to their home. They are given paper 36 by 18 inches to draw the map. They can try as many drafts as they feel necessary. To complete the map the students must observe and note the directions their school bus takes from school to their homes. Their maps are completed with as much detail as possible and are color coordinated. Maps may include a key and should be drawn reflecting a reasonable scale. Students are not graded on artistry. Maps will be displayed to the student body.

Number of Students: 25–30

Concepts:
1. Understanding a sense of place
2. Perspectives of the person in relationship to the space of a journey

Factual Information: All information placed on the map will be evaluated for factual correctness.

Skills:
1. Giving directions
2. Following directions
3. Observing the environment

Timetable of Activities:

TIME FRAME (BY WEEK/BY DAY)

(Day 1)   Topic assigned. Students begin maps and get materials. Observations begin on way home.

(Day 2)   Students continue work on maps based on the previous day's observations.

(Day 3)   Students continue work on maps, checking for accuracy on the way home.

(Day 4)   Students continue work on maps, checking for accuracy on the way home.

(Day 5)   Students submit final product at the end of class.

Evaluation: Teacher evaluation of maps for factual accuracy. Students evaluate their own maps in a short written narrative. Teacher takes sample of maps and spends one day driving to students' homes.

Corollaries to Murphy's Law: Joe Nowicki has found himself lost on an occasion or two. Enough said.

Course:	Geography
Length of Activity:	One week
Grade Level:	7–8
Unit:	Understanding Maps (final activity in this unit)
Topic:	Creating Maps According to a Set of Directions
Title:	Mapping Teachertown
Description of Activity:	Map Making

Overview: Cartographers both follow and give directions as they develop a perspective of where they are in relation to the rest of their environment. In this activity students are asked to draw a map of a fictitious town called "Teachertown" (Nowickiville). They are given a sheet of paper 36 by 18 inches to put the map on and a sheet listing fifty separate features such as landmarks, natural features, manmade features, and directions. Features are all named after members of the class. Students can try as many drafts as they feel are necessary and may add whatever they want to the map and create their own names. Maps may also be used to tell a story. Their maps are to be completed with as much detail as possible and color coordinated. Maps may include a key and should be drawn reasonably, reflecting a scale. Students are not to be graded on artistry. Maps will be displayed to the student body.

Number of Students: 25–30

Concepts:
1. Understanding a sense of place
2. Recognizing the idea of a perspective
3. Understanding how to use directions in one form to give directions in another

Factual Information: All information placed on the map will be evaluated for factual correctness according to the sheet.

Skills:
1. Giving directions
2. Following directions; cartography
3. Map reading

Timetable of Activities:

TIME FRAME (BY WEEK/BY DAY)

(Day 1) Topic assigned. Students begin maps and get materials.

(Day 2)   Students continue work on maps and share critiques with other students, working on individual maps yet together if necessary.

(Day 3)   Students continue work on maps and share critiques with other students, working on individual maps yet together if necessary.

(Day 4)   Students continue work on maps, checking for accuracy on each other's maps.

(Day 5)   Students submit final product at the end of class.

Evaluation: Teacher evaluation of maps for factual accuracy. Students evaluate their own maps in a short written narrative.

Corollaries to Murphy's Law: Joe Nowicki has found himself the central character in many of the maps.

Course: World History/Any geography course

Length of Activity: Two days

Grade Level: 9–12

Unit: Understanding Perspectives of Time and Place (first and last activity of the year)

Topic: Creating a Map of the World from Memories

Title: Mapping the World

Description of Activity: Map Making

Overview: Cartographers both follow and give directions as they develop a perspective of where they are in relation to the rest of their environment. In this activity students are asked to draw a map of the world as an introduction to the class. They are asked to imagine the world and then draw it. All other maps in the room are covered. Students are given an 18- by 36-inch sheet of white paper and have access to colored pencils. Approximately halfway through the first day of the exercise students are given a list of countries and natural features that they might wish to make sure their maps have. Each student must turn in their own map, and maps are to be collected at the end of class. The second day, maps are given back along with a new sheet of white paper. Students can use whatever maps they wish in evaluating and correcting their first work. Final maps are then collected.

Number of Students: 25–30

Concepts:
1. Understanding a sense of place
2. Recognizing the idea of a perspective
3. Understanding the importance of the physical
4. Understanding the importance of the political organization of the world

Factual Information: All information placed on the map will be evaluated for factual correctness according to the a current world map.

Skills:
1. Memory recall
2. Following directions
3. Cartography
4. Map reading
5. Developing an awareness of the world

Timetable of Activities:

TIME FRAME (BY WEEK/BY DAY)

(Day 1)   Topic assigned. Students begin maps and get materials.

(Day 2)   Students are given materials to evaluate maps and either correct old maps or construct new ones.

Evaluation: Teacher evaluation of maps for factual accuracy. Student evaluation of their own maps in short written narrative. (Note: Students have been asked to repeat this exercise on the last two days of school with varying results).

Corollaries to Murphy's Law: Students often assume that they know more of the world than they really do. Changes in political arrangement of the world hurt rather than help this activity, making it constantly more complex.

Course:	World History/European History
Length of Activity:	Two days
Grade Level:	9–10
Unit:	Understanding Perspectives of Time (supplement to a unit on nationalism and the rise of nation-states).
Topic:	Creating a Time Line of 19th Century Europe
Title:	Mapping Change Over Time
Description of Activity:	Time Line
Overview:	This strategy is meant to give an alternative perspective to a unit in World and European History. Students working in groups of three or four are asked to build a time line that includes at least 100 entries. Students are given a sheet of paper that is approximately 10 feet long and 3 feet wide. They are given access to coloring materials and whatever resource materials they may need, given the breadth of the materials available in the classroom and the school library. Time lines will be displayed when completed on the second day.
Number of Students:	25–30 (groups of three or four students working on one time line)
Concepts:	1. Understanding a sense of place 2. Recognizing the idea of time in developing a perspective 3. Understanding the importance of key events on the political organization of the world
Factual Information:	All information placed on the map will be evaluated for factual correctness.
Skills:	1. Mapping events 2. Developing themes and chronologies 3. Developing an historical awareness of the world
Timetable of Activities:	

TIME FRAME (BY WEEK/BY DAY)

(Day 1)   Topic assigned. Students begin time lines and conduct research.

(Day 2)   Students complete time lines and turn in completed work.

Evaluation: Teacher evaluation of time lines for factual accuracy. Student evaluation of their work in short written narrative.

Corollaries to Murphy's Law: Students not in school can jeopardize group work.

Course:	American Studies
Length of Activity:	Four weeks
Grade Level:	11–12
Unit:	Understanding Perspectives of Time (supplement to a unit on the 1960s in the United States)
Topic:	Creating a Time Line of the 1960s
Title:	Mapping a Decade of Change
Description of Activity:	Time Line
Overview:	This strategy is meant to supplement a unit in American Studies, focusing on the decade of the 1960s. Students working in groups of three or four are asked to build a time line that includes at least 200 entries. Students are given a sheet of paper that is approximately 10 feet long and 3 feet wide. They are given access to coloring materials and whatever resource materials they may need, given the breadth of the materials available in the classroom and the school library. Time lines will be displayed when completed and should reflect the creativity that three or four students can generate. Time lines do not simply have lines signifying events but may also use visuals. Students may also interview those who lived during the 1960s and elicit their perspectives.
Number of Students:	25–30 (groups of three or four students working on one time line)
Concepts:	1. Understanding a sense of place
	2. Recognizing the idea of time in developing a perspective.
	3. Understanding the importance of key events and the issue of change during a decade
Factual Information:	All information placed on the map will be evaluated for factual correctness.
Skills:	1. Mapping events
	2. Developing themes and chronologies
	3. Developing historical awareness of a decade
Timetable of Activities:	

TIME FRAME (BY WEEK/BY DAY)

(Week 1) Time line assigned. Students begin time lines and conduct research. One class day dedicated to time lines.

(Week 2) Students continue work on time lines. One class day allocated to time lines.

(Week 3) Students continue work on time lines. One class day allocated to time lines.

(Week 4) Students complete time lines. Products are displayed around classroom.

Evaluation: Teacher evaluation of time lines for factual accuracy. Student evaluation of their work in short written narrative.

Corollaries to Murphy's Law: Students not in school can jeopardize group work.

Course:	American Studies
Length of Activity:	Three days
Grade Level:	11–12
Unit:	Political Campaigns in the United States since 1944
Topic:	Creating a Political Advertisement
Title:	Vote for . . .
Description of Activity:	Advertisement

Overview: This strategy is meant to supplement a unit in American Studies focusing on the presidential elections of the past fifty years. Students working in groups of three or four are asked to create a political advertisement supporting the candidate of their choice from the possible list of people who ran for president. Advertisements can be videotaped, audiotaped, or can be in print or poster form. Students conduct one day of research and use another to produce their advertisement. Completed products will be presented on the third day.

Number of Students: 25–30 (groups of three or four students working on one advertisement)

Concepts:

1. Understanding the differences in American politics over time

2. Recognizing the linkages between policy and politics

3. Recognizing the importance of the vote in determining policy

4. Understanding how much a role advertisements play in determining elections and in constructing truth

Factual Information: All information placed in the advertisement will be evaluated for factual accuracy, given the information available at the time of the candidates seeking office.

Skills:

1. Producing an advertisement based on historical reality

2. Developing historical awareness of half a century

3. Research and production skills

Timetable of Activities:

TIME FRAME (BY WEEK/BY DAY)

(Day 1)   Students select candidate and begin research.

(Day 2)   Students construct advertisements.

(Day 3)   Students complete work and present advertisements. Elections follow at end of class.

159

Evaluation: Teacher evaluation for factual accuracy. Student evaluation of self and peers in short written narrative.

Corollaries to Murphy's Law: Students not in school can jeopardize group work. Campaigns can become competitive as students learn from researching actual campaigns.

Course:	World History
Length of Activity:	Two days
Grade Level:	9
Unit:	The Reformation/Renaissance
Topic:	Understanding the Time Limits
Title:	From Renaissance to Reformation
Description of Activity:	Time Line
Overview:	Students will work on completing a time line from 1350 to 1650. They are to look at issues in the Renaissance and the Reformation that were significant to the spread of each. The students need not limit themselves to written notations but may also use visuals and pictorials to represent key dates and events. Students use 2- by 3-foot sheets of display paper for the time lines; the teacher will supply various colored markers and materials. The final products are posted in the classroom for discussion and comparison.
Number of Students:	20
Concepts:	1. Cause and effect
	2. Relationships between parallel events in various cultures
	3. Comparison and contrasting
Factual Information:	The students will generate the key events; however, they must list a minimum of 25 events.
Skills:	1. Research
	2. Critical thinking skill
	3. Decision making
	4. Oral presentation
Timetable of Activities:	

TIME FRAME (BY WEEK/BY DAY)

(Day 1) Explain and assign

(Day 2) Complete project and post

Evaluation: The finished product will be evaluated with an emphasis on neatness, quality of product, significant number of events, and historical accuracy

Corollaries to Murphy's Law: As in many of the one- and two-day activities, absenteeism is a problem.

Course:	World History
Length of Activity:	Five weeks
Grade Level:	9
Unit:	The Medieval Period in Europe
Topic:	An Examination of the Medieval World and Its Culture
Title:	A Day in the Medieval World
Description of Activity:	A Day . . .

Overview: A Day in the Medieval World brings together the entire ninth grade class and engages them in a common activity composed of many individual and small group presentations. This activity is a supplement to the unit on the Middle Ages, although it can easily form the entire unit. The activity begins with students selecting topics concerning aspects of life and history from this civilization and its culture. For example, in this activity students have chosen to do their presentations on a particular period in world history. Their presentations focus on the religion, the various classes within the society, the language, the food, the music, the drama, the art, the technology, the features of the culture, and historical characters from the period. Much of the work is done outside of class, although various class periods are set aside for resource checks and progress reports. As the day of the festival approaches, students develop an outline of their presentation. This will include, but is not limited to:

1. Costume

2. Description of factual material and how it will be presented (maps, charts, graphs, pictures)

3 A sample of the hands-on material they will be using

4. A description of the demonstration they are designing for the day of a topic at which they have become "experts"

On the day of the festival students are given time to prepare their exhibits and demonstrations in the appropriate area, generally the cafeteria or the gym. Students will set up booths along the walls and create walkways for the visitors. Then at the appointed time, parents, students, and teachers are invited to the area, which now represents the fairgrounds at a medieval castle.

Number of Students: Approximately 90

List of Roles The member of the village the student is representing; possible characters include but are not limited to: a cooper, a blacksmith, the castle architect, a friar, an abbot, a knight, a squire, a page, jugglers, musicians, various serfs, lords, ladies, cooks, thatchers

Concepts:

1. The full knowledge of a historic culture

2. The division of labor

3. The process of developing a society

4. Greater understanding of the growth of classes

Factual Information:

Manor, manorial system, feudal system, elements of culture and civilization that create society, dates of Middle Ages, and other significant information that will be determined through research for inclusion in the presentations.

Skills:

1. Research skills

2. Subjectify important concepts of history

3. Assume historical persona

4. Oral speaking skills

5. Cooperative interdependence

Timetable of Activities:

TIME FRAME (BY WEEK/BY DAY)

(Week 1) Students select topics and begin independent research

(Week 2) One class day allocated for library work; students complete bibliography

(Week 3) One class day allocated for library work; students complete outline of presentation

(Week 4) Two class days allocated for library/preparation work; students complete outline 2 and updated bibliography

(Week 5) Two class days for library/preparation work; students complete final checklist of presentation, costumes props, materials, and format of presentation

Fair Day

Evaluation:

Teacher evaluation of all preliminary written materials and effectiveness of final presentation. Teachers and students outside of the class will complete a checklist evaluation sheet on various exhibits relative to thoroughness of information, creativity, thoughtfulness of demonstration, and amount of effort involved

Corollaries to Murphy's Law:

In any project of this magnitude there are always a number of areas where chaos can occur. It is imperative that students complete weekly assignments and updating of work; otherwise they fall into a hole from which it is almost impossible to escape. It is also important to make contact with various other departments within the school relative to the space needed for the fair and the time out of class on the final day.

Course:	American Studies
Length of Activity:	Five weeks
Grade Level:	10
Unit:	American Ways of Life
Topic:	Accepting Diversity in Culture
Title:	Native American Day
Description of Activity:	A Day . . .
Overview:	Native American Day brings together the entire tenth grade class and engages them in a common activity composed of many individual and small group presentations. The activity begins with students selecting topics concerning aspects of life and history from Native American civilizations and cultures. Their presentations will focus on the religion, the tribal structure within the society, the language, the food, the music, the drama, the art, the technology, the features of the culture, and historical characters. Much of the work is done outside of class, although various class period are set aside for "resource checks" and progress reports.

As the day of the festival approaches, students develop an outline of what their presentation will entail. This will include, but is not limited to:

1. Costume

2. Description of factual material and how it will be presented (maps, charts, graphs, pictures)

3. A sample of the hands-on material they will be using

4. A description of the demonstration they are designing for the day of a topic at which they have become "experts"

On the day of the festival, students are given time to prepare their exhibits and demonstrations in the appropriate area, generally the cafeteria or the gym. Students will set up booths along the walls and create walkways for the visitors. Then at the appointed time, parents, students, and teachers are invited to the area, which now represents a Native American village.

Number of Students:	Approximately 90
List of Roles:	Roles will be selected by the students.
Concepts:	1. The full knowledge of a historic culture
	2. The division of labor within the culture
	3. The problem of acculturation

4. An understanding of the use of differing technologies

5. Greater appreciation of diversity and richness in various cultures

Factual Information: Much of the factual material will come from the research of the Native American lifestyle and culture as the students prepare the presentation. However, they will look into the areas of government, division of labor, society, recreation, food, raising of children, migration patterns, and shelter and lodging

Skills:
1. Research skills

2. Ability to personalize and subjectify important concepts of history

3. Assume historical persona

4. Oral speaking skills

5. Cooperative interdependence

Timetable of Activities:

TIME FRAME (BY WEEK/BY DAY)

(Week 1) Students select topics and begin independent research

(Week 2) One class day allocated for library work; students complete bibliography

(Week 3) One class day allocated for library work; students complete outline of presentation

(Week 4) Two class days allocated for library/preparation work; students complete outline 2 and updated bibliography

(Week 5) Two class days for library work and organization; students complete final checklist of presentation, props, costume, materials and format of presentation;

Fair Day

Evaluation: Teacher evaluation of all preliminary written materials and effectiveness of final presentation. Teachers and students outside of the class will complete a checklist evaluation sheet on various exhibits relative to thoroughness of information, creativity, seriousness of demonstration, and amount of effort involved.

Corollaries to Murphy's Law: In any project of this magnitude there are always a number of areas where chaos can occur. It is imperative that students complete weekly assignments and updating of work; otherwise they fall into a hole from which it is almost impossible to escape. It is also important to make contact with various other departments within the school relative to the space needed for the fair and the time out of class on the final day.

Course:	World Geography
Length of Activity:	Three days
Grade Level:	7 or 8
Unit:	East Asia (or any other geographical or cultural region of the world)
Topic:	Understanding Elements of Life in Another Region of the World
Title:	Postcard
Description of Activity:	Students are given two blank 3 by 5 index cards, which they are to turn into postcards. On one side, students are to write a message and address the card to one of their teachers in the school. The message is to include five highlighted pieces of factual information that students have researched. The other side of the card is to represent a picture or design highlighting their fact-message as one would find on a standard postcard. They are to complete the activity with as much detail as possible and include such items as their own design of stamp and postmark.
Overview:	This activity links student research skills with the ability to report factual information in a conversational manner. It is a showcase for students to demonstrate their creativity. In particular, postcards progress from a simple fact-gathering activity to one that blends a number of complex skills into a final demonstration product. This activity encourages students to use their imaginations. The activity also encourages student and teacher links across the school community as the postcards, in final product form, are delivered to teachers. (In another twist this activity can take, postcards can be mailed to parents, grandparents, or others in the community).
Number of Students:	25–30
Concepts:	Understanding the relationship of geography and culture, recognizing how one can "view" a new culture or place as a tourist and the importance of "perspective"
Factual Information:	Minimum of ten direct facts (five per postcard) that deal directly with a geographical or cultural region in the world
Skills:	1. Researching
	2. Summarizing
	3. Writing to expand from simple factual material
	4. Artistic skills

Timetable of Activities:

TIME FRAME (BY WEEK/BY DAY)

(Day 1)   Students select topics, the activity is explained, cards are distributed.

(Day 2)   Students complete the activity.

(Day 3)   Postcards are distributed.

Evaluation: Teacher checks for highlighted facts. Teacher evaluation of overall effort. Students can evaluate their own work and explain the connections displayed on the card.

Corollaries to Murphy's Law: Often students want to do more than two cards. Some teachers in the school receive more postcards than others do.

Course:	World History/European History
Length of Activity:	Two days
Grade Level:	9–10
Unit:	Middle Ages/Renaissance/Age of Absolutism
Topic:	Recreation in the Past
Title:	Court Games
Description of Activity:	As a supplement to a unit on European History during the age of strong monarchs and ruling nobility, students will conduct research into the formal recreational activities, particularly the board games, played by members of the court. Once students can describe games, which may or may not have survived to this day, they will then engage in playing the games for one day.
Overview:	This supplemental activity brings the humanness of living to a study of a distant time and place. Students can play the same games as those in the past because one day of research is followed by one day of participation.
Number of Students:	25
Concepts:	The desire for recreation in all societies, the need to create diversions through games
Factual Information:	Historical documentation of activity found in court life, specific games, forms of entertainment
Skills:	1. Research
	2. Cooperative work skills in playing the games
	3. Organizing a demonstration

Timetable of Activities:

TIME FRAME (BY WEEK/BY DAY)

(Day 1) Teacher highlights activity and students research activity.

(Day 2) Students participate in a "game day" during class time.

Evaluation:	Student self-evaluation (written) and teacher evaluation (written or check-list)

**Corollaries to
Murphy's Law:** Students may often seek to choose the most difficult games. Students and teachers may demonstrate a competitive streak on game day. Some games may not be considered legitimate in the perspectives of our time and place.

Course:	World Geography, Western Civilization, World History, United States History, World Cultures
Length of Activity:	Three days
Grade Level:	7–12
Unit:	Particular to a subject area
Topic:	Scientific Advances Made by Each Civilization, Culture, and People During Specific Times of Their History
Title:	Scientific Experiments and Discoveries
Description of Activity:	During a particular unit based on grade level and course content, students, working in pairs, will conduct research into the scientific advancements of that particular cultural and historical period. Students conduct two days of research into the major scientific insights of the particular time and place that were gained through experiments. Students then duplicate the experiments in a third day class dedicated to sharing knowledge through demonstrations.
Overview:	This activity acknowledges the number of scientific contributions made by many peoples representing a diversity of cultures and of historical periods. Students conducting and replicating the same experimental procedures as others gain a sense of the importance of such experiments for the particular culture and historical time as well as for understanding the importance of scientific experimentation and its effects on technology and life for tomorrow's world.
Number of Students:	Two per experiment
Concepts:	1. The connection between culture and historical time to the development of scientific thought 2 The impact of history on scientific and technological development 3. The difficulty of scientific experimentation
Factual Information:	Specifically geared to the time of history, culture, or civilization under study
Skills:	1. Researching 2. Organizing 3. Demonstrating 4. Conducting and replicating scientific experiments 5. Working together in a paired activity

**Timetable of
Activities:**

TIME FRAME (BY WEEK/BY DAY)

(Day 1)   One class day dedicated to researching scientific experiments. Teacher sets the frame of reference by providing a written and detailed list of expectations for students on the first day.

(Day 2)   Students organize and begin experiments.

(Day 3)   Students demonstrate experiments.

Evaluation: Teacher evaluation based on checklist of student research and progress. Student self-narrative evaluation. Student pair evaluation of work on task.

**Corollaries to
Murphy's Law:** Students need to know that not all replications will be successful; emphasize that the method will be followed as closely as possible. It may be advisable to incorporate science teachers into the process or at least be able to secure space directly tied to experimentation in the physical sciences.

Course:	World History, Civilizations, United States History
Length of Activity:	Two days
Grade Level:	9–12
Unit:	War
Topic:	Warfare
Title:	Organizing the Troops
Description of Activity:	Students in a one-day class are given a large sheet of poster paper. Their instructions are to graphically chart the ways in which an army or navy is or was organized for the most efficient use of resources available. Organization can be geared to combatants in battles or wars as well as across the sphere of time. Three students work together on this activity, which should last two days.
Overview:	To enable students to understand the connections between organization and success or lack of success in military terms. Throughout the study of history, students hear about armies, battalions, or legions with a regularity that demands that students have some connection to the meanings behind these terms. This activity, shared by a class of students broken down into groups of three, allows students to graphically represent what they have been exposed to through course content and enables them to share their work with others in their class.
Number of Students:	Groups of three
Concepts:	1. The importance of organization in developing military discipline
	2. The importance of organization in developing efficiency and, at times, in retarding efficiency
	3. The changes and similarities of military organization throughout history
Factual Information:	Factual information geared to specific time and topic of study
Skills:	1. Researching
	2. Collaborative work
	3. Creating graphic representations
	4. Demonstrating knowledge gained through research to faculty and peers

**Timetable of
Activities:**

TIME FRAME (BY WEEK/BY DAY)

(Day 1)   Students conduct research and then build a flow chart representing a specific form of organization geared to their type and time of study.

(Day 2)   Students present work.

Evaluation: Teacher-generated checklist, teacher narrative developed in conjunction with student presentations, student self- and peer evaluation, teacher-generated test

**Corollaries to
Murphy's Law:**   A lack of immediately available research material can hurt this activity. The teacher may well have to plan for this before beginning the activity.

Course:	World Cultures, World Geography
Length of Activity:	Three days
Grade Level:	7–8
Unit:	Diverse Cultures
Topic:	How the Activity of a Race Is Used in Many Cultures
Title:	A Race
Description of Activity:	Students are exposed to the many types of traditions (competitive and noncompetitive) that are based on forms of "racing." These traditions are often culture bound. After studying a particular type of activity, students will then engage in the activity. Students must document the applicability and history of their particular form of racing in terms of another culture. Students in groups of five develop and plan a particular race and participate as a team.
Overview:	In this activity, students will encounter alternative and complementary understandings to their analysis of the idea of racing. The activities on which these ideas are based include standard notions of distance and time. They may also include, but are not limited to, the use of more than human means, such as chariots and horses or the racing of riders on camels. The activity links the knowledge and assumptions with the activities of other cultures while providing a complement to individual learning. The final activity consists of each group of students presenting their model and having other groups attempt to complete it.
Number of Students:	Groups of five
Concepts:	1. Recognizing the linkages that exist between cultures 2. The idea of time and distance as a form of competition or an obstacle in many cultures
Factual Information:	Information dedicated to specific cultures that reflect the idea of racing
Skills:	1. Working together 2. Making a presentation 3. Developing rules and presenting rules
Timetable of Activities:	

TIME FRAME (BY WEEK/BY DAY)

(Day 1)   Researching the topic of racing

175

(Day 2)   Research and group work at building a presentation

(Day 3)   Group presentations and, if possible, class/group participation in racing activities

Evaluation: Teacher-generated test, teacher-generated checklist completed by teacher, by student groups, and by individual students, evaluation of final demonstration

Corollaries to Murphy's Law: On race day it might rain.

Course:	United States History, World History
Length of Activity:	One day
Grade Level:	9–12
Unit:	Topics of Social Concern
Topic:	That Which Interests the Student
Title:	Political Cartoons
Description of Activity:	Students select an issue related to their area of study and draw a political cartoon representing a side to an issue. Their work must be original and cannot copy the work of another. Cartoons may incorporate current reflections on the historical topic as long as there is a sufficient amount of historical fact incorporated into the cartoon. Cartoons will be displayed in a gallery at the end of the activity.
Overview:	Cartoons offer students a great many ways of demonstrating their knowledge of the meanings represented by a particular historical event or of a particular issue.
Number of Students:	25
Concepts:	1. The use of satire as a form of social commentary
	2. The relationship of art to history and current events
	3. Specific historical concepts addressed through cartoons
Factual Information:	Factual information specific to the particular area of study though each cartoon must demonstrate the factual knowledge of the author.
Skills:	1. Historical analysis
	2. Researching
	3. Linking art to history
Timetable of Activities:	**TIME FRAME (BY WEEK/BY DAY)**
	(Day 1) Students work independently on cartoons and complete them for the next day's class
Evaluation:	Teacher evaluation, student self-evaluation, peer evaluation (Note: students not evaluated on artistic ability)

Corollaries to Murphy's Law: Some students will constantly attempt to draw cartoons along themes that apply to only today's world.

Course: United States History, World History

Length of Activity: Five to six weeks

Grade Level: 9–12

Unit: Exploration

Topic: As an Example: The Journal of a Western Fur Trader

Title: A Journal

Description of Activity: During a particular period of history dealing with the topic of exploration, either World History or United States History, students are required to write daily journals in which they attempt to take on the role of those members of exploration parties. The journals will be collected at the end of the unit and made available to the rest of the class. Students may also choose to write journals from the standpoint of those from existing populations who were forced to encounter "explorers."

Overview: Students will demonstrate an understanding of life as an individual engaged in exploration. Journal entries, with students taking on the role of expedition member, provide unique opportunities for visualizing history and making the events of the past personal to the students of today.

Number of Students: 25

Concepts:
1. Understanding the relationship of past to present
2. The relationship of an individual and a group to the environment
3. The importance of purpose to historical contexts of exploration
4. The importance of economics to the issue of exploration
5. The perspectives of those representing an existing society relative to the intervention of the explorers
6. Understanding various viewpoints about a particular topic

Factual Information: Subject specific, though all journals must have factual material to support entries

Skills:
1. Researching
2. Writing narrative
3. Incorporating factual material into particular reference points

Timetable of Activities:

TIME FRAME (BY WEEK/BY DAY)

(Daily entries checked weekly) Daily journal entries, double dated for historical and current accuracy

(Week 6) At end of unit journals are collected and reviewed by teacher before being made available to the rest of the class.

Evaluation: Teacher evaluation of journal entries by week and of final product.

Corollaries to Murphy's Law: Teachers need to make sure that students are current (even daily) with journal entries.

Course: United States History

Length of Activity: Two days

Grade Level: 10–12

Unit: Immigration and the United States

Topic: Reflections from the Immigrants About Their Experiences in the United States

Title: Immigrant Letters

Description of Activity: Students will write up to three letters per person, adopting the persona of an immigrant to the United States during the late nineteenth and early twentieth centuries. They are to do this during one class period and as a continuing homework assignment. The students may base their letters on a nationality or group, but they must write these letters in character and to those in their homeland. Letters may also be written from the immigrant's perspective to the rest of the people in the United States.

Overview: This type of activity provides a direct link between students and a time in our nation's past. It also offers a clear path toward understanding the issues facing immigrants today from the perspective of an immigrant.

Number of Students: 25

Concepts:

1. Understanding the issues facing immigrants

2. The differences in perspective between those vested in a place and those new to a place

3. The recognition that the experiences of immigrants, while seeming similar, do represent immense diversity

4. The understanding that equity was not a standard in the treatment of immigrants

5. Appreciation of the importance of economics in fostering and forcing immigration to take place

Factual Information: Immigration information as specific to the time, place, and population under study, as demonstrated in letters

Skills:

1. Translating factual information into representational dialogue

2. Conducting research

Timetable of Activities:

TIME FRAME (BY WEEK/BY DAY)

(Day 1)   Students write letters (continuing as a homework assignment).

(Day 2)   Student letters are made available for all in the class to read.

Evaluation: Teacher evaluation of letters for style and content

Corollaries to Murphy's Law: The teacher must make sure that all students know what is expected of them before the exercise begins and that the teacher offers a comment for all letters.

Course:	World Cultures
Length of Activity:	Three days
Grade Level:	7
Unit:	Africa South of the Sahara (or other cultural regions)
Topic:	Aspects of Village Life
Title:	Basket Activity

Description of Activity: Students in this class are arranged into cooperative groups. They are studying life in Sub-Saharan villages. Students have commented on the use of the head as a way of carrying cargo. To understand the unique and exceptional skills (in the students' culture) necessary for such an activity, cooperative groups are given a basket and assigned the task of carrying 2.5 pounds of cargo a distance of twenty-five feet. The activity should take two or three days and includes the measurement of how far baskets can be carried.

Overview: This activity ties the content in the unit students are studying with the realities of life in another part of the world. The activity speaks directly to the difficulty of life, given western cultural orientations, in another cultural area of the world. It stresses the importance and difference of physical skills in one culture as compared with another. All students are required to participate.

Number of Students: 20–25 (organized in groups of five)

Concepts:
1. Understanding cultural difference and uniqueness
2. Understanding the physical skills (fine and gross motor) used in another culture
3. Understanding how cultures and populations adapt to social and cultural demands

Factual Information: Peoples of Sub-Saharan Africa, weights carried by workers, elements of daily life in rural African villages

Skills:
1. Research into village life in Africa
2. Carrying the basket
3. Measuring the distance the basket is carried
4. Cooperative and collaborative work

Timetable of Activities:

TIME FRAME (BY WEEK/BY DAY)

(Day 1)   Students develop (in teams) plans for carrying the basket.

(Day 2)   Students carry baskets, individually, over a set distance.

(Day 3)   Students complete exercise of carrying baskets.

Evaluation: Peer, individual, and teacher, using checklist and narrative. Measurement of group or individual success is not the point of the activity but is rather a segue into the activity.

Corollaries to Murphy's Law: Students often find that such an activity is more difficult than they anticipate. Students need to address their own frustration levels.

Course: Western Civilization

Length of Activity: Two weeks

Grade Level: 9

Unit: Middle Ages

Topic: Growth of Technology During the Middle Ages

Title: Inventions of the Middle Ages

Description of Activity: During a three-week unit on the Middle Ages, students conduct research of technological contributions occurring during this period. Students will explain how these technological advances impacted the way people lived. The goal of the activity is for students to actually replicate inventions or create model demonstrations and then share these inventions with other students. An example of this activity could be seen in the development of the wheelbarrow in the High Middle Ages. Students may work as individuals or in groups of up to three, depending on the complexity of the task. They will be required to answer a question sheet on their invention, present a demonstration with rough plans, and provide a bibliography to document their research efforts.

Overview: This activity provides an opportunity for "hands-on" work and for students to experience the difficulty of building an invention, as well as understanding the impact of the invention, good or bad, for society. Not all inventions will be successful, and not all of the inventions, students will discover, met with lasting success to be carried on to our society. Using our previous example, the wheelbarrow, students will build a wheelbarrow.

Number of Students: 25

Concepts:
1. The impact of technology on society
2. The lasting effect of some inventions (in this example, how the wheelbarrow eased the tasks of laborers)
3. The negative effect of some inventions on social life (in some cases)

Factual Information: Size of the invention, shape of the invention, purposes, uses, impact on society, history of the inventor and the need for the invention, the time and place of the invention

Skills:
1. Research
2. Teamwork (in some cases)
3. Preparing a demonstration
4. Organizing a demonstration
5. Building a replica of an invention or a model of one

Timetable of Activities:

TIME FRAME (BY WEEK/BY DAY)

(Week 1 to day 2 of unit)   Activity is outlined with written expectations by teacher.

(Week 1 to day 4 of unit)   Students select a topic. One class during the week is dedicated to research. Teacher checks progress during and after class.

(Week 2 to day 6 of unit)   Students complete sheet listing progress and sources. Day 6 is dedicated to research activity.

(Week 2 to day 10 of unit)   Students demonstrate inventions.

Evaluation: Teacher checklist (throughout activity), student self-evaluation, peer evaluation at the end of the activity and during the demonstration

Corollaries to Murphy's Law: Students need clear expectations in the early set of directions and reinforcement as they continue with the task. If not monitored closely, the activity may not work. Students may also discover inventions that we find not always helpful for society. The teacher may wish to be aware of this possibility.

CHAPTER 5

The Trial

The *Trial Strategies* directly involve students in their learning experiences. Additionally, we believe that they significantly relate to the heterogeneous and cooperative classroom. We have divided the trial strategies into four areas: *debates, historical trials, mock trials,* and *point–counterpoint discussions.* In applying each of these strategies, our focus continues to be on the areas represented by concepts, skills, and facts, which are necessary components of every lesson. Likewise, we also continue our focus on opportunities for evaluation that the classroom teacher might wish to consider.

AN OVERVIEW OF TRIAL STRATEGIES

Our lives are a constant set of *trials.* Whenever more than one of us has a better solution for a particular problem, we have the basis for a *trial.* That shared problem can be as simple as two people trying to find the best way to change a washer in a leaky faucet or as complicated as developing a policy that will have enormous national implications. In both cases, and in the myriad of others we encounter every day, we put our ideas and the ideas of others *on trial.* At times one or two people present us with *evidence* from which we make a *decision.* We must be *objective* in our decision making and base our decision on *facts* presented by one or both parties, or from our own experiences. Through our involvement in trials we learn to present our arguments and frame our judgments according to a set of agreed-on *rules.* These rules may be as simple as treating one another with mutual respect or as complicated as those that define the process of bringing an appeal to the United States Supreme Court.

Teachers use, or should use, trials all the time. But often the use is informal and not recognized as a learning strategy within itself. Trials are formal strategies that can become either the centerpiece of a unit or can serve in a supplemental role. As learning strategies for the classroom, trials contain the fact finding of interview strategies and display the knowledge evident in demonstration strategies. They take the process of the classroom one step further by encouraging students to present arguments and to critically appraise information according to agreed-on rules. Although staging a trial may appear to some to be only a demonstration of student product, we disagree. As a set of learning strategies trials are vivid examples of the processes inherent in how we learn and think in action.

A Note About Heterogeneity

Trials are not only learning strategies that contain concepts, facts, skills, and a form of evaluation, but they can be a powerful motivator for students engaged in collaborative and cooperative activity. They represent the most applicable learning strategy for the heterogeneous social studies classroom because the trials in our courtrooms and the issues in our municipal and local elections are tried before a heterogeneous audience. Additionally, the writings of historians and biographers leave us with a wealth of information and insights that we often deem the province of only "top students." However, our experience suggesting that information is accessible by all students prompts us to question the concept of designated top students. Activities such as those we present here clearly show that top students are those who are motivated by the activity, not those randomly assigned through intelligence quotient or socioeconomic background. Consequently, we need to develop the critical skills that will enable *all* members of our community to present arguments and make sound and rational decisions.

Competition

We believe competition is healthy and useful to motivate students. The trial strategies produce competitive situations within a classroom. These are not situations in which one individual wins and another loses. We have designed the strategies in this chapter to produce collaborative and cooperative learning experiences in which a group, or team of students, finds themselves arguing a point, a case, or the value of one idea against another. The people on a team work together during one experience. At another time, and during a separate activity, students are working in reconfigured groups. It is the teacher's responsibility to continue a mix of the groups so, as in any cooperative learning activity, work groups do not always contain the same people. As always, teachers are guides.

   Although students may find themselves competing as members of one group against another, our focus as teachers is not on the competition but on the progress the students are making and in what they are learning. We also believe that it is our responsibility as teachers to monitor the levels of competition that naturally develop when two groups propose alternative interpretations. Our duty is to encourage students to reach alternative accommodations and a synthesis of ideas, just as we are responsible to be sure that those engaged in the class activity follow rules of propriety.

The Issue of Age Appropriateness and Expectations

Groups of students from the middle school and junior high school years through senior high school can apply each of the trial strategies that follow. The teacher sets expectations for detail within the activity with age as a consideration. To be sure, the level of sophistication or the length of an activity differs according to the age of students taking part. Yet the models we have created in this chapter are applicable to any classroom. The teacher must set limits of time and content that are age appropriate.

SPECIFIC STRATEGIES

In providing an overview of each of the categories of trial strategies, remember the strategies are not rigid and set in stone but rather are fluid so the individual classroom teacher can adjust them to his or her needs. As all teachers know, there is no final draft. We continually change, adjust, and modify the activities in our repertoire. Many teachers will find there are components of our trial strategies in activities they use. That gives credibility to these strategies rather than negates them. After all, we all continually search for the teaching strategy that most effectively meets the needs of our students.

Debates

This strategy is a part of our culture. It has become formalized and ingrained into clubs and societies that fill our schools. As our national and world leaders debate the fate of our society, we seek answers from the process. Yet we at times we ignore debate's potential for our classes. As we will show, debates can frame a wide number of activities that take place in the social studies classroom.

Trials of Historical Characters

The breadth of history offers an unlimited number of individuals who could be brought to trial. This chapter will present one specific strategy of a *trial of a historical character*. It also includes a suggestion list of possible trials, with our recommendation of age appropriateness. To be sure, this is far from being a conclusive list. There can never be such a list, given the breadth of human experience.

Mock Trials

These strategies describe the use of trial formats in bringing a character to a trial in a manner that replicates the legal procedure we follow in society. Based on a knowledge of local and state law, each trial deals with fictitious characters from popular culture or characters the classroom teacher creates. These strategies are different from those presented in the historical trial because the mock trial deals with the fictitious rather than the real. These strategies also involve a greater procedural knowledge of the law.

Point–Counterpoint

Cooperative and reflective of our society, this strategy most resembles the process by which we negotiate the realities in which we live. As a classroom strategy, it demands that one participate in creating a proposal, making a response, and forming a new proposal. The strategy takes content from the realm of social studies and integrates it with the world of all learners. As with the other strategies in this section, our list is only a list of ideas and is incomplete.

PROCEDURES FOR TRIALS

Trials can function either as the foundation of a unit or as an activity to supplement the standard curriculum. Holding a trial can be a powerful way of integrating the material of a course with the day-to-day world of a student's life. Trials also offer invaluable opportunities for starting cooperative learning experiences or for building on the collaborative ideas proposed by other strategies that we have highlighted in this book.

Some Basics

This section outlines two types of trials, but they follow a very similar format. Many teachers now use trials, and some very good ones are in textbooks for high school law courses, in supplemental texts, and in publications from state bar agencies and associations. We have geared the two types of trials we highlight in this chapter to heterogeneously grouped classes of social studies students. We have found that ability distinctions tend to fall apart when students engage in trials as members of cooperative and competitive teams and learning groups.

The trials and examples of trials that we suggest follow the basic plan for all mock trials. The teacher's plan or blueprint needs to be flexible enough for the teacher to make adjustments for the age level of a class.

Elements

All trials have two sides. One side represents the defense, and one side acts as either plaintiff or prosecution, depending on whether the case is *civil* or *criminal*. This chapter gives examples of both. Depending on the type of trial, students may need to make an arrest and conduct an investigation, developing evidence to bring to court.

The trial itself can take place in a time limit designed by the teacher to meet the needs of the class. For example, middle and junior high school students cannot develop the sophisticated trials of seniors in high school. But the expectation for both groups undertaking a trial exercise includes the specific steps in preparing and presenting a case.

An Outline of Steps (both trials)

I. The teacher presents the outline of the case and assigns witness/ attorney roles. Students who will be portraying witnesses for both prosecution/plaintiff and defense complete typed statements that represent their testimony (In the historical trial they include footnotes and a bibliography highlighting their information; mock trials also involve other activities, which are included in the notes section after this outline). The students and teacher exchange the statements or depositions and establish a certain time for the case to go to court. One copy of each statement is placed as a part of the book that represents the products of the class.

II. Opening Statements

 A. Prosecution (criminal cases), Plaintiff (civil cases) goes first. This statement should tell what this side plans to do with its case.

 B. In both cases, the defense makes the opening statement, explaining what they will try to do. The students submit all typed statements from both Defense and Prosecution/Plaintiff.

III. Presenting the Prosecution or Plaintiff's argument. This includes a direct examination of witnesses representing this side and then a cross-examination of witnesses representing the defendant. Again all questioning from both sides is typed and submitted.

IV. Presentation of the Defendant's argument. This will include a direct examination of witnesses representing the Defendant's position.

V. Closing statements by lawyers representing each side. Again students submit typed statements to the teacher.

VI. Jury deliberations consider all the evidence presented by both sides throughout the trial. In the absence of a jury, the trial judge will reach a decision.

VII. The presiding judge writes and submits a typed copy of the final decision.

VIII. All materials are now collected, printed, and bound for a class record of the trial.

Notes

1. In the case of mock trials, a videotaped record of the trial is beneficial. We use this format both for a record and for student self-peer and teacher evaluations.

2. Because of the time constraints, the time allotted for any case can vary. Time limits for opening and closing statements as well as for direct and cross-examinations must be limited. A ratio of five minutes for statements, seven minutes for a direct examination, and five minutes for a cross-examination usually works and can be adjusted to fit the needs of the class.

3. Social studies teachers unsure of this format because of a lack of knowledge of legal procedure and terms can find the information through many readily available local and national sources. However, the main point is students are learning a process, and, as with any process, refinement comes with repetition. Don't be afraid to experiment.

4. The expectation is that all students participate. When students realize their grade reflects their efforts, cooperation, and involvement, the issue of affective grading becomes very important.

5. Mock trial strategies are based on fiction, and historical trials are based on historical events. Although the trials are closely paralleled, our mock trial strategies also include elements not included in the design for historical trials. For example, mock trials usually include the following additional steps:

    a. A crime is committed.

    b. An arrest procedure, including police questioning that leads to later testimony, occurs.

    c. Physical evidence is accumulated if possible.

    d. Depositions are taken from characters not testifying (this is in case other voices from outside the class might be needed).

    e. We always try to use a jury of peers in a mock trial case. Jurors are selected on a voluntary basis from other social studies classes, from a sample of students in study hall periods, and from available administration and faculty.

6. In both trials, the teacher needs to be *the* guide.

Objections and Technicalities

1. Students need to learn the difference between a leading and a direct question. Leading questions are allowed in our trials and in those of our court system during the time one side is allowed to cross-examine the other side. A direct question is allowed during the time one side speaks to witnesses representing their own side.

2. We have handled objections to questioning and testimony in the following way, which can vary depending on the age level of the class:

    a. Hearsay testimony is not allowed.

    b. Long narrative answers are not allowed.

    c. Any contradiction between testimony and typed statements can result in a witness's testimony being impeached.

    d. Only relevant material to the case is allowed.

    e. All evidence must be submitted for inspection by both sides at least two days before a trial.

    f. Whether an opinion should or should not be allowed during testimony is up to the discretion of the presiding judge.

    g. Expert witness distinction is made by the presiding justice. Arguments must be made for and against by both sides.

h. A judge is usually selected from a pool of students who have taken the class the year before. In unusually difficult cases, a knowledgeable faculty member has served as a judge.

i. We guarantee that there will be many difficult questions raised to the teacher who is guiding this activity. Students want rulings. It seems they want a world that is black and white, when in reality it is rather gray. In cases in which there is no established practice to fall back on, the teacher is encouraged to create a new "local rule" to remedy the disagreement.

j. We cannot overstate how important it is for the classroom teacher to set the direction for the trial. These experiences should, above all, fit the needs of class.

We begin with an example of a mock trial that Joe has used for seven years. We have included a sample of some of the roles that have been written into this case, along with a list of other mock trial possibilities. We believe that it is important enough to stress again that this activity is *flexible* and *fluid* and should be designed to fit the needs of teachers and students.

*Sample
Trial
Strategies*

Type of Activity:	Mock Trial
Unit:	Introduction to Criminal Justice System
Grade Level:	11–12
Title:	The Trial of Gold E. Locks
Number of Students:	20–24

Overview: The teacher assigns this case at the beginning of the first unit of the course. As the course progresses, students have opportunities to work on their parts. Usually, the trial date is scheduled for the sixth or seventh week into the unit. Students schedule all aspects of the case, such as warrants, complaints, arrest, booking, and conducting an investigation.

Students can elect to serve either on the prosecution or the defense team. In a class of twenty, the students realize that each side will have ten members. The teacher presents students a list of characters who will be depicted in the case for their role selection. If they cannot decide on a role, the teacher will assign one. Each side will have four attorneys and six witnesses to call.

ATTORNEYS' RESPONSIBILITIES

Attorneys for each side are responsible for preparing and conducting all direct examinations of their witnesses and cross-examinations of the witnesses on the opposing side. In addition, the group of attorneys provides an opening and closing statement. Students taking on the role of attorney work cooperatively with the witnesses they represent in designing effective and appropriate questioning. Attorneys also must work in a cooperative fashion as they develop an opening statement for their side and work on a closing statement during the case for presentation as their summary. At the conclusion of the trial, each attorney submits a typed copy of their questions and statements. Attorneys may use any material while questioning or delivering statements.

WITNESSES' RESPONSIBILITIES

All students serving as witnesses become the character they represent. Based on the available information, witnesses complete typed statements of their testimony for the court. In their statements they cannot contradict any of the information that is provided to them, and they will be held to their statements in court when testifying. Their statements will be shared with the other side at a specified time before the trial and will become part of the case book. Opposing attorneys may also interview the witnesses if they choose to do so. The witness may have his or her own attorney present. Police officers conducting an investigation of an alleged crime may also interview and question the witnesses. Witnesses *will not* have access to their statements while on the witness stand.

CASE MATERIAL

The teacher is responsible for providing all the factual material the students need for their statements. For this particular case, a copy of the tale *Goldilocks and the Three Bears,* from the children's section of a local library, frames the case. All students are required to read this version of the story. The teacher also supplies a narrative for the fictitious roles with information not contained in the story. This additional material allows for character development. Sample narratives follow.

VIDEOTAPING, THE JUDGE, THE BAILIFF, AND THE JURY

We have held our trials in classrooms and in the school library. Our librarians, who are also our media people, have always been invaluable in helping us conduct a successful case. Trials are videotaped so they can be used for assessment and to encourage student self-critiquing.

A student who had taken the class in the past or who has some other experience with the trial process usually plays the role of judge. Occasionally, a student from the class has taken on the role. The judge is responsible for making all rulings that affect the court, including setting codes for behavior and dress if that person so desires.

A teacher always takes on the role of bailiff. During the case it is the bailiff's responsibility to insure that the judge's decisions are upheld and that the sacredness of the courtroom is respected.

Our juries come from a random selection of students in the school who have a study hall during the period the case is heard. They also include faculty and administrators as members. On occasion the juries have also been large, such as when composed of an entire social studies class at an earlier grade (for example, a junior high school class studying Civics).

EVIDENCE

Students submit whatever evidence they wish as long as the evidence does not contradict either the story line or the narratives assigned to students. For example, police officers may wish to submit arrest reports, videotapes of interrogations, and fingerprint records, among other things. With the judge's permission, physical evidence is also submitted.

WITNESS ROLES

Defense	Prosecution
Gold E. Locks	Papa Bear
Mr./Ms. Locks (1 parent)	Mamma Bear
The School Teacher	Baby Bear
The Nurse	The Police
The Local Beekeeper	The School Principal
The Hiker	The Town Gossip

Each of these witnesses must know the tale that frames the case. Yet in the story there is not enough background information to allow for the complete development of student statements. A character such as Goldi Locks and the members of the Bear family have plenty of material for their statements. Similarly, the police officer who must conduct the arrest, file charges, follow the procedures, and complete the forms (available from most local police departments) has enough information for a statement.

Other characters need some additional material, however. This is where the teacher adds to the narrative and creates supporting roles in designing the case. *The object is to create a case that can be both prosecuted and defended.* How the story line is altered is up to the teacher and can depend on the class and the age level of the students. Some brief examples of story lines Joe has used are:

Papa Bear, Mamma Bear, and Little Baby Bear:

Most of your testimony will center on the trial's main script. You must also write out a sworn statement for the court, which must agree with the main script. In particular:

1. You must be interviewed by the police because you filed the complaint and reported the crime.

2. The police must take a statement from you.

3. Your statement must be recorded with the court, and you are held accountable for everything that you say.

4. Your statement should be at least two pages long.

5. You must remember that the suspect is someone who you want found guilty. You must remember that the suspect has disrupted the serenity and lives of you and your family.

6. Lastly, your testimony must agree with that of your family members and with the script. But remember that you moved to this town to do "Bear things" such as live in the woods, go to the Teddy Bear picnics, escape the crime and problems of your last home, let your child go to school, and be wild and free. If you ignore these things, your case will suffer.

The Police Officer:

You are responsible for:

1. Identifying yourself

2. Working with your Prosecution team (remember that you want the suspect put in jail and away from the rest of society)

3. Coming up with a two- to three-page police report that will be entered as evidence in court and will be shared with others involved in the case

4. Your police report:

   a. Must include the time of the complaint and what you did to respond

   b. Must include what took place during your investigation. Be sure to note times, dates, and witnesses

   c. Should not include your own opinions

   d. Must include taking statements

   e. Must have charges to be brought against the defendant

5. You must do whatever is required to arrest and bring a suspect to trial (this is a team effort).

The School Principal:

As the Principal of the school, you will include the following into your expectations:

1. You will not deviate from anything involved in the trial script.

2. You must prepare a two-page statement that will be shared with members of the legal teams from both sides. In other words, you must be responsible for what you claim to be evidence.

3. As principal, you found Goldi to be a constant and continuous behavior problem (you are expected to expand this into at least a paragraph). Goldi and Baby Bear have had problems in your school since the Bear family moved into town.

4. You will need to establish your credibility as a witness and the relevance of your work in this case.

The Town Gossip:

You are responsible for a two- to three-page statement, which will be shared with the court and which must agree with the rest of the script for the trial. You also must agree with the rules of name, address, and age, and whatever other information is required to make you a credible witness.

As the Gossip, you may add:

> For a year you have wondered about Ms./Mr. Locks and that kid Goldi. You remember the parent from the days you went to school together. That person wouldn't give you the time of the day then, and always seemed to be better than you or most everyone else. You know about the problems at the school between the teacher and the principal, and you have heard talk that Goldi is really a spoiled and conniving kid who would stab you in the back if you were not looking. You have seen her a lot, just hanging around town dressed in those dirty clothes, and you know that she has just been up to no good. It was not a shock when you heard her name on the scanner. You were glad that they finally got her.

The School Nurse:

1. You are bound by the case script.

2. You are expected to provide information about age, address, and so on.

3. You know that Goldi comes from a family that is not in the upper economic status of the town. You know that Ms./Mr. Locks has been unemployed and has lived from odd job to odd job. You also know that you saw Goldi and that she was cut, bruised, and suffering from the latter stages of shock and hypothermia. You need to write a two- to three-page report about your observations, having seen Goldi four hours after the first police report was filed.

Goldi:

You are to subject yourself to being the arrested suspect in a felony case. The prosecution must describe charges that they are pressing. You must come up with interviews and a two- or three-page statement explaining why you were in the Bear house and what you were doing there. Remember, you must stay with the script.

Goldi's Parent:

1. Your child has been framed.

2. The Bear family (new to town) is trying to cause trouble.

3. You are a poor family trying to make ends meet, and you must deal with those rich Bears.

4. You will talk about your child as being a tremendous and helping child.

5. You will talk about Baby Bear as constantly picking and beating on Goldi even though Goldi tries to ignore the abuse.

6. You are expected to have a two- to three-page statement about why your child is not guilty.

Teacher:

1. You are a teacher in the junior high school. You have both Goldi Locks and Baby Bear in class. It has been a difficult fall for you. Goldi was always one of your best students. But this fall, Goldi's performance has slipped a bit. She seems angry and at times distracted. Often Goldi looks very tense.

2. Part of the problem has been Baby Bear, the new child in your class. Baby has been picking on Goldi and other children since entering school. Goldi has been Baby's particular target. You think that is the reason why Goldi has been doing so poorly.

3. Also, you wonder if Goldi is getting enough to eat at home because Goldi looks tired and worn out. You know that her parent is having a tough time making ends meet financially.

4. The Principal and you do not get along. You have taught at the school for ten years. The principal has been around for only five. Although you and Ms./Mr. Locks are best friends from high school days, the Principal and Ms./Mr. Locks do not agree on anything. When you tried to tell the principal about the problems caused by Baby Bear, you were told that "Baby Bear doesn't have a problem; you do because you play favorites in class and can't control the behavior of school-age children."

Hiker:

1. You are a get-back-to-nature kind of person, and as such you spend hours, even days, outdoors. You enjoy hiking and climbing and spending time at outdoor shops. Oftentimes you hike from your home in one town to another town miles away and return for a little walk. Always you

keep to the deep woods with your official and stylish backpack, boots, and wardrobe.

2. On the day in question, you were bounding up a trail in town, heading back home, when you saw a girl who looked tired, wet, and bruised off in the woods. It was about 10 o'clock in the morning. The sight seemed odd to you, an expert woodsman, and you tried to catch up with her because you were worried about her condition.

3. It is up to you to describe what you saw in the woods. You did not talk to her up close, though you did yell to her. She may have yelled back as she ran away. You came home, called the police, and later identified Goldi's picture as the child in the woods.

Beekeeper:

1. You have been a beekeeper for over fifty years. Your little business off in the woods south of town has always made you enough to live comfortably. Your honey is so pure it is in demand worldwide. You know everyone in town, though you do not take to all the new people. Too often the people in all those new houses zap your bees with pesticides.

2. Lately though, business has not been that good. Your hives have been broken and tipped over, resulting in the loss of a lot of honey. Though you have not caught the culprits, you have your suspicions. Off in the woods you have noticed a number of small bear prints, and you do know about that new Bear Family. You have heard the stories about Papa Bear. You have also seen kid Bear making poor little Goldi Locks cry right in front of your house as they wait for the school bus some mornings.

NOTES

The Mock Trial is a strategy that involves all students in a cooperative and collaborative venture. We have suggested one example of application, but the possibilities for different scenarios are endless, as are the modifications that can be made to this strategy.

Concepts:
1. An understanding that the purpose of a trial is to bring out the truth

2. Guilt needs to be proven beyond a reasonable doubt

3. There are defenses that can justify what may appear to be a crime

4. An understanding of the arrest process and the rights of the accused

5. The knowledge that an attorney presenting the prosecution's argument represents the state, and we, as citizens, the make up the state

6. The knowledge that a defense attorney represents a client

7. A concrete understanding of the relationship between the Bill of Rights and the trial process

8. The difficulty in reaching a unanimous decision

9. The impact of interpretation on the decisions of the law

Facts: The trial process, reasonable doubt, opening and closing statements, direct and leading questions, warrants and the arrest process, questioning and the rights of the accused, verdict, the jury system, the role of a judge, objections such as hearsay, relevance, impeachment of evidence, affidavit, perjury, testimony, under oath, the Bill of Rights, defendant, prosecution, plaintiff, Miranda Warnings, cross-examination, direct examination, redirect and recross examinations

Skills:
1. Presenting a cooperative argument with many segments
2. Drafting statements
3. Interviewing
4. Taking depositions
5. Questioning
6. Critical thinking skills

Time: The mock trial format allows students five minutes for opening and closing statements, seven minutes for direct examinations, and five minutes for cross-examinations. Attorneys may ask up to three redirect and three recross questions. The teacher may have to adjust times to insure that the trial is completed within a week.

Although the trial itself lasts a week in this format, it is flexible enough to be altered to either a shorter or longer time. As stated at the beginning of this section, trials such as this one are prepared throughout the unit and serve as a culminating part of the process. It is up to the people of the class to establish a time table and to hold each other to it. Usually part of one class or, as the trial progresses, one class a week are dedicated to work on the case. Once again, this is a flexible issue.

Evaluation: The evaluation is based on three elements:
1. A teacher evaluation of each participant's performance
2. Student self-evaluation and peer evaluation through reaction papers, watching the case videotape, and reading the class-constructed book of case documents
3. This activity promotes student growth and development. Although students are graded on what they demonstrate, the evaluation should also take into account the creative and personal growth experience inherent in the strategy as well as intellectual mastery of factual material. Again, the affective grade is important in activity-based learning.

Age/Grade Expectations: This strategy can be used in classes at the middle school, junior high, and senior high school. It has also been used in even lower grades, with appropriate modifications for that particular class.

Corollaries to Murphy's Law: Students need to be in school to make the strategy work effectively. We have seen students demanding that peers be present because of their desire to put together a solid case. Many students are anxious about taking the witness stand but then are amazed at their efforts. Students also always seem to be excited about seeing themselves on tape.

List of Possible Topics: Here are other mock trials we have used following the same strategy and format. They are based on fiction. Some require the creation of roles; others, as in the case of Shakespeare, rely directly on the text of a play.

TOPIC	GRADE LEVEL
The trial of Hamlet for murder	9–12
The trial of Brutus for the murder of Caesar	9–12
Shylock sues Antonio for defamation of character	9–12
The trial of Hansel and Gretel	7–12
The trial of the Three Little Pigs	7–12
The trial of Little Red Riding Hood for conspiracy	7–12
The trial of Peter Pan for kidnapping	7–12
The trial of the Fox for eating the Gingerbread Boy	7–12
The trial of the Grinch	7–12
The trial of Jack (as in the beanstalk story)	7–12
The trial of Santa Claus for breaking and entering based on Clement Moore's "A Visit from Saint Nick"	7–12
The trial of Chicken Little for disturbing the peace	7–12

The list could go on and on and can be added to with self-designed creations or with any of the available guides.

Type of Activity:	Historical Trial
Unit:	American Studies/American Revolution
Grade Level:	10–12
Title:	The Trial of George Washington
Number of Students:	20
Overview:	This strategy presents a historical trial. The design is to follow the process already outlined for the trial as a general strategy and the mock trial. The difference between historical trials and mock trials is there is no arrest process. The charges are on file, and the experience begins directly in the courtroom, though there is ample time for preparation. This strategy assists in teaching a special unit rather than representing the unit itself.

In this case we have resurrected George Washington in our society, and we are to try him on charges brought by several individuals in signed complaints. Today's students are to pass judgment on George Washington based on his actions in the period from 1775 through 1781. The trial will last a week, will be videotaped, and the court documents will produce a case book.

From a class of twenty, eight students fill the roles of lawyers who conduct all direct and cross-examinations and deliver opening and closing statements. Four students represent the prosecution, and four represent the defense. Copies of the work produced by the lawyers are included in the case book. Prosecution lawyers must list the charges filed against the defendant.

Twelve students serve as witnesses; six of these will be called to support the defense, and six will testify in support of the prosecution. The witnesses represent actual historical characters, who submit a three-page typed statement to serve as the basis for their testimony. The statements are the products of student research. These statements come from historical documents and other historical research. The students may use any source of information, but any statement of fact is footnoted and included in a separate bibliography page. Both prosecution and defense have an opportunity to review the statements. Attorneys and witnesses work together in developing lines of questioning. Witnesses *will not* have their statements available while on the witness stand, though attorneys *will be able to use* whatever materials they wish during questioning and delivering statements. (For this example, witnesses will be listed and assigned to a specific side. But in the actual class trial, students will have an opportunity to select their personae.

LIST OF WITNESSES

Prosecution	Defense
King George III	John Adams
General Thomas Gage	George Washington
General William Howe	Thomas Jefferson
General Henry Clinton	Ben Franklin
Benedict Arnold	Abigail Adams
A Tory living in New England	John Hancock
Widow of an executed Tory	Martha Washington

EVIDENCE

Students submit whatever evidence they wish, as long as the evidence comes from footnoted actual sources identified in the bibliography. The judge will determine submissibility of physical evidence.

OBJECTIONS

Objections follow the same abbreviated set of rules described in the introductory sections describing the trial as a strategy. The acting judge in the case always decides objections.

VIDEOTAPING, THE JUDGE, THE BAILIFF, AND THE JURY

The same procedures and justifications as stated in the mock trial apply for the historical trial.

Concepts: This trial represent two content areas of learning. The information is *historically grounded.* It also represents an *understanding of law* and the concepts that frame our process of justice.

HISTORICAL CONCEPTS

1. The rationale for engaging in a revolution

2. The implications of the Declaration of Independence

3. The importance of Washington as a strong leader

4. Understanding the negative feelings of the British and of Tory sympathizers living in the colonies toward the revolution

5. The feelings of a woman in a male-dominated Revolution

6. The comparison inherent in the use of today's attitudes in evaluating events of the past

LEGAL CONCEPTS

1. The trial process

2. The idea that apparent criminal actions can be justified under our law

3. The search for truth according to a set of mutually accepted rules

4. The importance of framing a cooperative and collaborative argument

Facts:

HISTORICAL AND UNIT CONTENT

An activity such as this can generate a multitude of facts because of the implications and possibilities that come from researching history. The case book will be a source of facts, including the footnote and bibliography additions, at the end of the activity, and it can lead to further discussion of issues such as the American Revolution, the Declaration of Independence, the role of women during the Revolution, Tories, Patriots, and specific characters, battles, geographic places, and events.

LEGAL CONCEPTS (RELATED TO THE TRIAL)

The trial process, reasonable doubt, opening and closing statements, direct and leading questions, questioning and the rights of the accused, verdict, the jury system, the role of a judge, objections such as hearsay, relevance, impeachment of evidence, affidavit, perjury, testimony under oath, the Bill of Rights, defendant, prosecution, plaintiff, cross-examination, direct examination, redirect, and recross-examinations.

Skills: Historical research, developing statements, creating a cooperative argument, asking questions, critical thinking and assessing of information, creative writing, factual writing, public speaking

Time: The case could be a two-week activity in which research and trial occur as a total class focus, or it can be stretched out over the course of a unit, with trial preparation using one class per week. The trial then lasts one week of dedicated time. If the need arises, the teacher may shorten the trial by limiting the number of witnesses, though it is advisable to incorporate all students in the activity. The thrust of these activities is toward cooperative and collaborative activities, and these demand total involvement from all members of a class.

Evaluation: The evaluation is based on three elements:

1. Teacher evaluation of each participant's performance

2. Student self-evaluation and peer evaluation through reaction papers, watching the case videotape, and reading the book of case documents

3. This is meant to be an activity that promotes student growth and development. Although students are graded on what they demonstrate, the evaluation should also take into account that this strategy is an experience that provides for creative and personal growth as well as for intellectual mastery of factual material.

Age/Grade Expectations: This strategy can be used in classes at the middle school, junior high, and senior high school. It has also been used in even lower grades with appropriate modifications of the strategy.

Corollaries to Murphy's Law: Students need to be in class. Occasionally there is a small reaction about the material covered in that it forces people to address their own perspectives. The trials can become competitive.

List of Possible Topics:

TOPIC	GRADE LEVEL
Trial of Julius Caesar for creating a dictatorship	9–10
Trial of Abraham Lincoln for using excessive force	10–12
Trial of Carrie Nation for destruction of property	11–12
Trial of a sports figure such as Johnny Pesky for holding the ball during the 1946 World Series	11–12
Trial of Charlemagne for usurping the authority of the Pope	9–10
Trial of Senator McCarthy for defamation of character	10–12
Trial of Mao Tse Tung for crimes against humanity	11–12
Trial of Chiang Kai-shek for crimes against humanity	11–12
Trial of Harry Truman for crimes against humanity	11–12

This is but a short list and it can be extended as much as and to the degree permitted by the time available to the subject and classroom teacher.

DEBATE: A POWERFUL TOOL FOR LEARNING

A debate is an activity in which teams compete against each over an agreed-on issue. Each side tries to convince the audience to adopt what it considers to be a more effective solution to a problem. The debate is an excellent opportunity for students to learn to research a topic, identify the key issues, and recognize there are two sides to most issues. Debate is a powerful way for students to take control of their education as they decide major points and prepare formal written summaries that effectively argue a position. Debate teaches students to use examples, facts, and statistics to support their ideas and to disprove an opponents' statements. Debate teaches students to argue an issue using research and logic, not emotion.

The debate can be a very formal affair, with three to five members on a team who proceed according to guidelines for debating, or it can be as simple as two people arguing a position in a point–counterpoint situation. The degree of sophistication is up to the teacher, who knows the capability of the class. Remember we are adjusting the debate to a classroom situation, not preparing a debating society. Kerry has successfully conducted debates for many years with students of various ages.

The activity begins with the wording of the proposal. The wording must be specific to show clearly two opposing sides. One side, the affirmative, supports the proposal; the other side, the negative, opposes the adoption of the proposal. The agreed-to wording of a topic about accepting a government based on the adoption of a newly created constitution might state:

> *Resolved:* The adoption of the new Constitution is necessary for the establishment of a United States of America.

The affirmative will argue and show why they believe the country should adopt the new Constitution. The negative side will show that the Articles of Confederation, although not without problems, is still the better form of government and consequently oppose or negate the affirmative's belief in making the change.

Some Practical Hints in Running a Debate

1. State all propositions as the status quo, for example:

   Gun control is not necessary in the United States.
   Abortion is an issue of choice.
   Twenty-one is an acceptable drinking age.

2. Set realistic time limits for the speakers. What may be excessive for some classes is too short in another.

3. If this is the first time for debate with the class, take them very carefully through the preparation stage. The hardest part for them is to use research, logic, and inference rather than emotion.

4. Daily checks are necessary to keep students on task; if they fall behind, the results are devastating.

5. Videotape all debates; it is a powerful motivation to do well. Remember, all high school students want to look good.

6. If possible, show the class a videotape of a debate or have a local debate club from a local college come in and present a modified debate to the class. Most students today have never witnessed a formal debate.

7. Students need to realize that it does not matter which side of the issue they are debating; the importance of debate is experiencing the process of logical argumentation. Kerry has even waited to assign sides to an issue until a week of research has been completed. This method ensures that students look globally at an issue rather than at only the perceived "right side." Thus, by the time the sides are selected, it is not a big deal.

8. For a formal style of debate, the following guidelines are effective for most 40- to 45-minute classes. However, these are only suggestions; again teachers are the best guides to establish the structure for the individual class.

   Speaker 1: First Affirmative (7 minutes)

   Speaker 2: First Negative (7 minutes)

      Short break

   Speaker 3: Second Affirmative (7 minutes)

   Speaker 4: Second Negative (7 minutes)

      Short break

   Speaker 5: Negative Rebuttal (5 minutes)

   Speaker 6: Affirmative Rebuttal (5 minutes)

In summary, we have found that debate is a valuable addition to the social studies teacher's repertoire. It does so many of the things that we want kids to do. It totally involves them in the activity because they have to examine all sides and nuances of an issue to prepare successfully for the opposition. This leads to multiple perspectives developing as the students see that many issues are not as simple or clearcut as they want them to be. Additionally, research is an activity that places the responsibility of learning on the student. Because debate de-emphasizes a right or wrong answer, students must come to their own conclusions and accept ownership of that position. Consequently, they learn not only subject matter but responsibility, civility, critical listening, and thinking. Hopefully, the process encourages them to be less dogmatic and more open minded. Exploring issues in a logical and reasonable fashion is a valuable tool for an informed and critical citizenry.

Sample
Debate
Strategies

Type of Activity:	Debate
Unit:	Forming the New Government: The Constitution
Grade Level:	10
Title:	Resolved: The adoption of the new Constitution is necessary for the establishment of a United States of America
Number of Students:	24
Overview:	*Compromise* was a very important word at the Constitutional Convention. Many of the colonial states had written constitutions of their own that granted freedom and independence to their citizens. These constitutions showed the desire of the citizenry to have a voice in their own government. The Articles of Confederation were the first attempt to establish some sort of national government. Yet some saw this as a failure because there were no binding laws nor was there a clear separation of powers between the central government and the states. Consequently, the delegates to the Constitutional Convention in Philadelphia who had been called together for "the sole and express purpose of revising the Articles of Confederation" faced many issues regarding the creation of the government.

This topic lends itself quite easily to debate. The affirmative side is charged with the responsibility of proving the *need*, the *practicality*, and the *desirability* of the ratification of the new constitution. The negative side will champion the Articles of Confederation and offer arguments in support of the Articles. They may admit there are some problems with the existing articles, but they maintain that the basic ideas of the Articles are most important. They will show that the ideas of the new constitution are not valid or responsive to the needs of the growing country.

The debate will then address the major issues that led to heated and spirited debate in Philadelphia more than 200 years ago. Students will face the complexity of such issues as a strong/weak central government, sectional issues, slavery, regulation of commerce, the ability to raise a central army, equal representation, and taxes.

There are a number of ways this debate could be set up.

- **Option One:** In a class of 24 students, break the class into eight groups of three, which will lead to four debates. Each of the four debates addresses a different issue facing the convention. For example, the first debate will focus on the powers of the central government, the second debate will address the slavery issue, the third debate will square off over the equal representation problem, and the final debate will grapple with trade, commerce, and taxation. In this format, limit the major speeches to three minutes and the rebuttals to two minutes. This allows time for two debates in a standard 40- to 45-minute class.

- **Option Two:** In a class of twenty-four students, simply break the class into two large groups; one is for the adoption of the constitution, and the other group is against it. Each student within the groups assumes the persona of one of the original members of the convention. Each student is responsible for researching the role and developing his or her feelings over the major issues. These students then supply the research for the three to five principles they would choose to debate their issues. After completing the research, the standard debate format is followed.

- **Option Three:** Again appoint each member of the class to a role from the original conventioneers. Students will have a certain amount of time to research the character and write a one-page position paper on the topic most important to him or her. The students will then participate in a full debate, with one student serving as the chairperson. All students have to speak at least once but are limited to a three-minute speech. At the end of the allotted time, the convention will vote on the issues.

Concepts: The concepts involved in a debate are twofold. One deals with the historical information and ideas involved in the discussion. The second area stresses the debate techniques of logical argument and discussion.

HISTORICAL CONCEPTS:

1. The constitution is basically a series of compromises

2. The nature of a republic

3. Government as the continuum that struggles to maintain the balance between order on one side and chaos on the opposite

4. The elastic clause

5. The principle of adaptability

6. Federal unions versus individual liberties

DEBATE CONCEPTS:

1. The complexity of many issues

2. Multiple perspectives

3. Civility

4. Respect

5. Collegiality

6. Nuances of ideas

Facts: Articles of Confederation, Constitutional Convention, May 14, 1787, 55 delegates, Declaration of Independence, major figures such as Benjamin Franklin, Thomas Jefferson, James Madison, George Washington, Alexander Hamilton, Patrick Henry, the Great Compromise, the Three-Fifths Compromise, the commerce compromises, the Federalists, the anti-Federalists, franchise, electors, *The Federalist,* delegated powers, reserved powers, shared powers, separation of powers, Bill of Rights, treason, bill of attainder, civil liberties, ex post facto, writ of habeas corpus, judicial review

Skills: 1. Methods of research

2. Ability to see the "big picture"

3. Argumentation skills

4. Compare and contrast various pieces of research

5. Discrimination in selection of supporting data

6. Using inferential skills

7. Ranking the importance of information

8. Differentiating between fact, opinion, and emotion

9. Deductive reasoning

10. Listening skills

11. Oral presentation

12. Thinking on one's feet

13. Refutation

Time: Depending on the amount of available time, the teacher may choose to make the debate the full unit on the constitution. Therefore it could easily last two to three weeks. The teacher could easily extend the unit by following up with a second debate in which the students, now armed with a knowledge of debate and government, hold their own constitutional convention to write a constitution for the school. This could extend the unit a week or more but would certainly require synthesis and application to better understand the issues of forming a government. Conversely, a teacher could easily complete the debate in one unit with four days for research and one to two days for the debate(s). One of the benefits of debate is this adaptability of the format to the class and to the time constraints teachers must consider.

Evaluation: Evaluation can take many forms in a debate. An immediate evaluation for the participants is the result of the debate, "Who won?" This is decided either by having the audience vote on the winner or by completing a rating scale to determine the winner. Other aspects of evaluation include written briefs and outlines that the participants prepare for their speeches, amount of time and effort involved, and their success in establishing relevant points. The videotape is also helpful to reexamine individuals' performances. Additionally, having the students grade themselves and the other team is also a very informative and a helpful tool.

Age/Grade Expectations: As stated earlier, debate can work at any level. Students enjoy arguing and need to learn to argue using logic, facts, and inference rather than emotion. Once students master the framework, all age groups from seventh to twelfth grade can effectively debate. All ages need a tight pattern to follow, especially in the early going. In the younger grades, we have found two-person teams with two speeches and one rebuttal work well; in the older grades, three speeches of longer duration with two rebuttals are

215

easily handled. Start small and work up. Handled correctly, debate is one of the most satisfying and exciting activities to use in any social studies classroom.

Corollaries to Murphy's Law:

Be organized the first time. Because debate may be new to students and demands a certain tight framework, the teacher must exude confidence both for the class and in the activity. Be careful of time; too much time and the debate loses its zest, too little and students feel unnecessary pressure because of the public nature of the presentation. Also, student absentee-ism is a real killer. Affective grading for cooperative efforts, responsibility, and dedication to the final product is a must.

LIST OF POSSIBLE TOPICS:

Topic

1. Resolved: The United States should vote to accept membership into the League of Nations.

2. Resolved: The German people should vote to accept the conditions of the Treaty of Versailles.

3. Resolved: Julius Caesar should cross the Rubicon River with his troops and enter Rome.

4. Resolved: All 19-year-old's in the United States owe mandatory public service to the country.

5. Resolved: Execute all followers of Spartacus.

6. Resolved: Grant Julius Caesar the title of "Emperor," with all the associated powers.

7. Resolved: Expand the freedoms contained in the Magna Carta to include all peoples of Great Britain.

8. Resolved: Grant absolute power to the President of the United States.

9. Resolved: The economic policies of Adam Smith are the foundation of the United States government.

10. Resolved: Declare Napoleon Bonaparte as the Emperor of France.

11. Resolved: Mandatory education is required of all students until they reach the age of 19.

12. Resolved: Communism should be the accepted form of government in the United States today.

13. Resolved: It is the duty of the United States to enter World War I against the forces of German imperialism and militarism.

14. Resolved: It is the duty of the United States to enter World War II against the imperialism, militarism, extreme nationalism, and tyranny of Adolf Hitler.

15. Resolved: It is the duty of the United States to enter the war against the aggressive imperialism and militarism of the Japanese.

16. Resolved: Award Adolf Hitler the Nobel Prize for his statesmanship in leading Germany out of the chaos and depression of World War I.

17. Resolved: The United States should drop an atomic bomb on Hiroshima to end the fighting and Japanese imperialism.

18. Resolved: The United States and its allies should use military force and advanced military weaponry against the country of Iraq.

19. Resolved: The Jews receive the land known as Israel for a permanent homeland.

20. Resolved: All states entering the union from this point on continue the institution of slavery.

21. Resolved: Elect Martin Luther to the position of Pope of the Holy Roman Empire.

POINT–COUNTERPOINT

The point–counterpoint strategy is a very effective tool to stimulate classroom discussion as well as to foster higher-level thinking skills. It demands that students take ownership of their thoughts, put them out in public for discussion, yet learn to listen and change. This is an excellent foundation for the theory building, the highest order of critical thinking, which we should be encouraging and providing within the social studies classroom.

The process for point–counterpointing is relatively easy and a one-day process. The teacher presents an idea to the class, for example, *President Harry Truman's decision to drop the atomic bomb on Hiroshima was the correct decision to bring about the end of World War II.* One half of the class agrees with the proposal and the other half takes the opposite side. After agreeing on the wording of the proposal, students write a one-page defense of their side of the issue for homework. In class the next day, students each pair with a student who supported the opposite side. The students read their defenses and argue their ideas with each other. These ideas become the springboard for the larger class discussion. As a follow-up activity, the students will write a one- to two-page personal statement on the proposal that is the result of their research, thinking, sharing, listening, and rethinking. This way students are reinforcing the integrative thinking skills so important in the acquisition of knowledge.

Type of Activity: Point–Counterpoint

Course: American History

Unit: World War II

Title: President Harry Truman's decision to drop the atomic bomb on Hiroshima was the correct decision to bring about the end of World War II.

Grade Level: 10

Number of Students: 20

Overview: The issue of President Harry Truman's decision to drop the nuclear bombs on Japan to end World War II has been a hotly debated and controversial decision for years. Although some historians believe that Japan was close to surrender and that this destruction of civilian life was totally unnecessary, others argue that the Japanese people never would have surrendered, dragging out the war, with a staggering loss of life on both sides. Consequently, there are two very different and recognizable sides to the issue. Both sides can support their position with sound reasoning and inferential thinking.

Concepts:
1. The burdens of leadership
2. The toll of war in human lives
3. The beginning of the Nuclear Age

Facts: Hiroshima, Nagasaki, Russian declaration of war against Japan, specifics of devastation of the bomb on Hiroshima: 60 percent of the city destroyed, no buildings left standing within four miles of the center of the blast, 80,000 killed, 37,000 injured, many others died later of radiation effects, August 15, 1945—"V-J Day," September 2, 1945—surrender signed.

Skills:
1. Critical thinking
2. Researching
3. Inferential thinking
4. Listening skills
5. Writing
6. Oral presentation skills

Time: Two days

Evaluation: Emphasis in the evaluation is on the written defenses of the proposals. Comparing defenses with the personal statements of others forms an interesting part of the evaluation. After the discussion, students write a one-page narrative explaining what they learned and specifying any changes in their thinking as a result of the discussion.

Age/Grade Expectations: This activity is easily adaptable to any grade level from 7 to 12. The degree of sophistication in the rationale is relative to the grade and the expectations.

Corollaries to Murphy's Law: It is very important that the issue chosen be one with clearly identified sides. If it is ambiguous, the clarity of student thinking and supporting rationale are weaker.

Type of Activity: Point–Counterpoint

Course: American Studies

Unit: The Revolutionary War

Grade Level: 10

Number of Students: 20

Title: The American Revolution Was an Unnecessary War

Overview: Was the American revolution necessary? Or was the revolution merely the result of emotional ideology of a few influential men who were capitalistic and anti-monarchy? Why did the colonies want independence, yet Canada found no reasons for revolution? This is the issue to clarify to involve the class in the Revolutionary War unit. Too often the students think the rule of the crown was oppressive because of the democratic views students have from our contemporary society. This exercise has students confront the issue of the day from the point of view of 1775 and objectively examine both sides of the "treason" or "fight for liberty."

Concepts:
1. Declaration of Independence
2. Revolution
3. Principles of taxation
4. Differing forms of government
5. Rights of humans
6. Rights of governments
7. Capitalism

Facts: The Sugar Act of 1764, Pontiac's Rebellion, the Proclamation of 1763, the Currency Act of 1764, the Quartering Act of 1765, the Stamp Act of 1765, the Townshend Acts, writs of assistance, the Boston Massacre, Committees of Correspondence, the Tea Act of 1773, George III, John Adams, Sam Adams, Lord North, the First Continental Congress

Skills:
1. Critical thinking
2. Research
3. Close reading and inferential skills
4. Listening and interpreting
5. Written and oral presentation skills

Time: Two days

Evaluation: Emphasis in the evaluation will be on the thoroughness and use of supporting information for the rationale in the written defense of the proposal. Copies of student statements are anonymously distributed to those taking the other side for reaction papers, which are read, discussed, and collected.

Age/Grade Expectations: This proposal can be used in eighth grade social studies or any American Studies history class.

Corollaries to Murphy's Law: More specific wording of the proposals is very important to eliminate confusion or ambiguity.

LIST OF POSSIBLE TOPICS:

World History

1. Capitalism is an effective economic policy that benefits most citizens.
2. The United States today is a modern Athens.
3. Mandatory public service should be required of all 19-year-olds in the United States.
4. The United States today is similar to the latter stages of the Roman Empire.
5. The Magna Carta was a major step in guaranteeing the rights of humans.
6. Should schools encourage Humanistic thought today?
7. Martin Luther was a heretic who should have been tried for crimes against the Church.
8. An absolute ruler would be a better form of government for the United States today.
9. Terror is a very effective means of establishing control and order within society.
10. Communism is a better form of government than democracy.
11. The Theory of Social Darwinism is valid and constructive.
12. Nationalism and militarism lead to racism and bigotry.
13. Hitler was an effective and visionary leader.
14. Harry S. Truman should have been charged with war crimes and placed on trial for the decision to drop the atomic bomb.

United States History

15. Material considered pornographic as defined by community standards should not be protected by the First Amendment.
16. The United States entered World War I to protect its economic investments in certain European countries.

17. The United States government's handling of Indian affairs was tantamount to genocide.

18. Were it not for his assassination, John F. Kennedy would be remembered as a mediocre president.

19. Operation Desert Storm was fought to guarantee an ample and cheap supply of oil to the United States.

20. The United States should have used nuclear weaponry in Vietnam.

CHAPTER 6

Strategy Four: Building Theories

OVERVIEW

This final set of strategies deals with *theory building*. These strategies represent a concluding set of applications for the classroom teacher that build on the interviews, demonstrations, and trials presented in preceding chapters. In fact, these initial strategies function as foundation blocks to the art of *building* a *theory*, a more complex critical thinking skill involving both application and synthesis. Consequently, this chapter represents learning at the highest order while presenting a description of a strategy that is accessible to *all* learners regardless of attributed ability or age.

MAKING SENSE OF THE WORLD

We construct theories every day. Our lives are made up of creating frameworks that explain or justify some aspect of our social and physical lives. Our theories can offer us simple solutions to mundane problems or complicated intellectual constructions that deal with the most complex and challenging dilemmas we face. Sometimes our theories are valid and sound, and at other times they do not satisfactorily answer our concerns. Consequently, either what we create remains a constant source of explanations to which we tenaciously hold, or, after closer testing of our theories against those of others, we find it necessary to create alternative explanations. In this manner, our theories help us to make sense of and justify our world.

Our experience, in both the affective and cognitive domains of life, demands that we establish personal theories on which we continually build. These theories are based on what we encounter and observe within our world. The world of the social studies classroom is no different. In fact, the classroom is the place where we should gain the knowledge to build theories, present them to the world of our peers, and submit them to the litmus tests of challenge and debate.

The Integrative Side of a
Student as a Theorist

When students are asked to frame theories as a part of a conscious process, they must integrate knowledge of facts, understandings of concepts, and mastery of specific skills. While learning the process that will allow them to shape the way they organize and interpret knowledge to make sense of their current and future world, theory building also sharpens students' critical thinking skills. Through this struggle with ideas, students learn that what they think and speak is important. Furthermore, they can operate from a position of seeing the "big picture" rather fragmented historical data that do not appear to have immediate relevance to them. Additionally, it forces students to confront the societal view rather than to operate from the myopic view of adolescent self-interest. If we are to educate students for the next century, as so many educational and political leaders tell us, then we must create a generation of people comfortable with thinking beyond the personal, standard, and accepted. We need to develop people who both have an understanding of the theory-building process and are able to follow that process in shaping the future.

The Individual and the Group:
Cooperation and Collaborative
Theory Building

The earlier types of strategies we presented focused on the cooperative and collaborative possibilities for students in both the preparation and the presentation of work. Theory building is not an exception. Although an individual ultimately creates the constructions and makes the connections that lead to his or her understanding a segment of life, those constructions reflect what is gained through a cooperative and sharing experience. Consequently, we firmly believe that theory building should not be limited to what is produced by the individual. It should also focus on what can be produced by the large or small group. The importance of the individual is then celebrated by the process of group work and at the same time the individual is held accountable to the group for acting as a contributing member. Furthermore, we have found the heterogeneity of cooperative work groups enhances the creative process for *all* students.

Integrating Student Research into the
Art of Theory Building

In earlier chapters we presented numerous strategies that included important research components. We have presented "researching" as an important skill for all students to master. Teaching only those students in the "college track" the process of research is a serious educational error with profound consequences later in life. Learning how to investigate and to follow rules that govern investigation are important skills. These skills not only have application in the working/ blue collar world but are necessary to have an informed and responsible citizenry who are capable of making difficult choices affecting society.

The importance of research parallels the importance of theory building. As we have stated earlier, theories are important to all learners and to everyone who can be expected to cope successfully with the increasing complexity of everyday life. But research and theory building not only are parallel components of learning but are linked in an inseparable relationship. The more complex and developed the learning experience, the tighter the linkage.

Discovery

The celebration of discovery is at the essence of the relationship between theory building and research. Nothing is more exciting for a teacher than watching a student, working individually and with others, follow the process of conducting an investigation into a topic of interest and then construct a valid theory to explain the discovery. As the student discovers his or her process and conclusion, the rise in self-worth and esteem is overwhelming. Therefore, we believe it is essential for classroom strategies to lead a student to express a discovery, no matter how small or mundane it may seem to others. This should be in the form of a well-thought-out theory. In this sense, the social studies material is integrated by the student into a framework through which it can be understood and have new meaning in a larger relationship.

SHORT TERM, LONG TERM, AND THEMES

The strategies describing theory building that we present represent both long-term and short-term processes. We leave the actual length of a particular strategy to the discretion of the individual classroom teacher. The complexity of the experience is likewise reflective of the amount of time the teacher can budget as well as the age group of the class. We hope that theories are the last step in a process of learning and exploration that begins with and is built on the strategies outlined in this book.

The examples of theory building that follow show how they can be incorporated into the short-term realm of a unit or activity spanning a few weeks. Building theories can also be the culmination of a much longer period of study, such as multiple units or a semester or year course. In these instances, theories incorporate, represent, and explain common themes that run through a unit, a semester topic, or a year-long course.

In our theory strategies, we have given examples of the complete process. However, this is again up to the individual teacher as to how he or she chooses to follow the plan. Students can be given any part of the process, and they are then expected to fill out the full plan. In other instances, the teacher could give the students the theory on which to build. For example, *Extreme nationalism fosters racism and bigotry.* The job of the class is to examine the unit and find examples from the interview, the demonstration, and the trials that either prove or disprove this theory. Or it can function the opposite way. The teacher may say, "Based on your analysis of *Mien Kampf*, the Holocaust, and the war crimes trials, what can you determine about human behavior?" The number of ways a teacher may choose to use these are almost unlimited; however, the key is the final step. Students create or prove/disprove a theory based on the knowledge they have gained. We believe there are rewards. We have seen our students take responsibility for their learning, gain a process, and develop ideas. In using these strategies, we have seen our students learn to be learners and thinkers: lifelong survival skills.

Samples of
Theory Building
Strategies

INTERVIEW

Strategy: Thought question: Should society sacrifice personal freedom to protect against chaos?

Topic: Julius Caesar

Skill: Interviewing techniques

Concept: The need for dictatorship

Fact: Caesar became dictator to save Rome.

DEMONSTRATION

Strategy: Museum: Guillotine, Bastille

Topic: French Revolution

Skill: Preparing a demonstration, making an artifact

Concept: Terror as a means of social control

Fact: Reign of Terror

THE TRIAL

Strategy: Debate

Topic: Czar Nicholas declares that unrest should be put down.

Skill: Debate techniques; research

Concept: Military force used to preserve the order of the Nation

Fact: Bloody Sunday

THEORY (STUDENT CREATED)

Theory 1: Force is necessary to maintain the order within society.

Theory 2: Chaos in society is the result of the iniquitous use of force and distribution of wealth.

Time Frame: One year

Course: World History

Notes: This is an example of both a summarizing activity and a long-term theme.

INTERVIEW

Strategy: Thought question: How would you function if the supply of petroleum products your household uses was cut in half?

Topic: Natural resources

Skill: Interviewing; questioning; reporting

Concept: Lifestyle is linked to supply of resources.

Fact: The United States imports more than half of the oil it needs.

DEMONSTRATION

Strategy: Who Am I's? (leaders of OPEC)

Topic: OPEC leaders respond to the issue of overconsumption of oil and of dwindling resources.

Skill: Role playing, research

Concept: There is a finite amount of oil.

Fact: Oil use is not decreasing worldwide.

THE TRIAL

Strategy: Point–counterpoint

Topic: The industrial world's use of military power to protect OPEC's oil reserves from another nation's aggression

Skill: Research, questioning, presentation of argument, critical thinking, responding to an argument

Concept: Military involvement is often dictated by economics

Fact: The G-7 nations have been involved in protecting Mid Eastern oil fields.

THEORY (STUDENT CREATED)

Theory 1: Scarcity of resources can produce conflict.

Theory 2: The world economy shows the interdependence of nations.

Time Frame: Three weeks

Course: World Geography

Notes: Part of a larger unit on either physical or cultural geography

INTERVIEW

Strategy: Thought question: Do all citizens have an obligation to serve their country?

Topic: Obligated government service

Skill: Interviewing techniques, writing, and organizing

Concept: Government service, nationalism, extreme nationalism

Fact: Compulsory military duty (the draft)

DEMONSTRATION

Strategy: Time line: Create a time line of the military draft throughout its history in the United States

Topic: The military draft

Skill: Research, organization

Concept: Obligated governmental service has been expected throughout United States history.

Fact: The draft ended in the waning days of the Vietnam war.

THE TRIAL

Strategy: Point–counterpoint

Topic: All nineteen-year-olds owe one year of obligated government service.

Skill: Research, inferential thinking, oral presentation, and argumentation skills

Concept: Obligated government service

Fact: President Clinton proposed a form of mandatory service to the country.

THEORY (STUDENT CREATED)

Theory 1: To remain a free and democratic society, all citizens need to donate a year of their life in service to their country.

Theory 2: In a free society, individuals have the right to choose whether to serve the country or not.

Time Frame: One week

Course: American Studies

Notes: This particular activity is a very effective summarizer. It is best studied after students have studied the end of the draft during the Vietnam era. At this point the students have a historical frame of reference to use for their theory building.

INTERVIEW

Strategy: Interview: An interview with Adolph Hitler based on the ideas presented in *Mein Kampf* (Note: in a class of twenty, ten students will take the role of Hitler, and the other ten function as interviewers)

Topic: Adolf Hitler's ideas on racial and ethnic differences

Skill: Comprehension and interviewing strategies

Concept: Hitler's belief in Aryan supremacy is based on ideas of racism

Fact: The Holocaust, the rise of the German nation after World War I under Hitler's leadership, Adolf Hitler wrote *Mein Kampf*

DEMONSTRATION

Strategy: Time line: Hitler's rise to power, with an emphasis on the religious and ethnic persecution in Germany

Topic: The Holocaust

Skill: Research and organizing material into a time line

Concept: Humanity's inhumanity to one another; humans' indomitable will to survive; the need to learn from the lessons of the past

Fact: The Holocaust, the beliefs of racial supremacy

THE TRIAL

Strategy: Historical trial

Topic: The trial of Adolph Eichmann for crimes against humanity

Skill: Historical research, developing statements, asking questions, assessing information, creative and factual writing, inferential thinking skills, oral discussion and presentation skills, thinking and responding in a trial situation

Concept: The evil of human actions, the abuse of power, the danger of blindly following orders

Fact: The Holocaust, Adolf Eichmann, the Nuremburg trials

THEORY (STUDENT CREATED)

Theory 1: Extreme nationalism can foster racism and bigotry.

Theory 2: Hitler's policies restored pride among the German people as they rebuilt Germany after World War II.

Time Frame: One week

Course: World History

Notes: This is a good activity to work on during the World War II unit. It allows students to directly deal with the evil in humanity and examine the rationalizations for that evil. This type of theory building can apply to many other war situations. It is easily applicable to the Bosnian and Northern Ireland unrest of today.

INTERVIEW

Strategy: News report

Topic: The assassination of the Archduke Ferdinand

Skill: Historical research, interviewing techniques, videotaping

Concept: Nationalism was a leading cause of World War I.

Fact: Gavrilo Princep, a Serbian Nationalist, assassinated the archduke and his wife

DEMONSTRATION

Strategy: A Day in Sarajevo

Topic: Understanding the feelings, emotions, and pride involved in creating the feelings of nationalism

Skill: Researching, role playing, organization

Concept: Nationalism is the feeling of pride in a group of people who share language, customs, traditions, and lifestyle.

Fact: The Serbian people had been overtaken by Austria-Hungary.

THE TRIAL

Strategy: The trial of Gavrilo Princep for the assassination

Topic: Causes of World War I

Skill: Historical research, interviewing, preparing statements, assuming roles of historical personae, inferential skills, preparing and arguing a case

Concept: Nationalism as a major cause of war

Fact: Gavrilo Princep assassinated the Archduke, and war was declared within weeks.

THEORY (STUDENT CREATED)

Theory 1: Nationalism was a major cause of World War I.

Theory 2: Nationalism is a powerful force in world relations.

Theory 3: Imperialism and militarism cannot subdue the feelings of nationalism.

Time Frame: One week

Course: World History

Notes: This is a tight unit. You can begin with any one of the theories or all three and have students prove or disprove them. Or the alternative is that after examining the information gained in the three strategies, students will arrive at and defend their own theory.

INTERVIEW

Strategy: News report

Topic: The invention of movable type

Skill: Historical research, role playing, organization, creative writing, videotaping or audiotaping, sequence of material

Concept: The invention of movable type altered the development of civilization.

Fact: In the mid 1400s Europeans were using movable metal type to print a book; Joannes Gutenberg, a German, printed the first book, a Bible.

DEMONSTRATION

Strategy: Museum; students will create a museum of writing techniques using various forms of creating written words and symbols. Artifacts range from hieroglyphics to movable type to modern-day computers.

Topic: The development of the printing press rapidly increased the spread of knowledge.

Skill: Research, knowledge, and use of writing techniques

Concept: Universal truths and ideas are spread through reading; historical documents and contracts have a profound impact on civilization, written language is essential to civilization

Fact: There have been many different forms of writing and printing throughout the ages.

THE TRIAL

Strategy: Point–counterpoint

Topic: Modern society demands that all members be computer literate to effectively function in today's world.

Skill: Research, inferential skills, creative writing, effective use of facts to support ideas

Concept: Technology drastically alters the communication level of society.

Fact: Computers exist in almost every facet of everyday life, from automobiles to banking to schools.

THEORY (STUDENT CREATED)

Theory 1: Technology plays a major role in the development of civilization.

Theory 2: Technological changes in written language have the greatest impact on education and standards of living.

Time Frame: One week

Course: World History

Notes: This is also a very good summarizing theory building activity. Students have finished the year's work, and this forces them to go back over key technological developments to put all the pieces together to recognize the impact of current technological advancement.

INTERVIEW

Strategy: Documentary

Topic: Art and literature through the ages

Skill: Comparison and contrast; selection of appropriate materials, interviewing techniques, videotaping, researching, assuming historical personae

Concept: Art and literature reflect the society that creates them.

Fact: Every era has examples of great art work that portray society.

DEMONSTRATION

Strategy: Time lines/museum

Topic: A cultural perspective

Skills: Research, creating artifacts

Concept: A study of one's art and literature reveals a great deal about the values of the civilization.

Fact: Cave drawings, pyramid drawings, castle architecture, oil painting and sculpture, DaVinci, Michelangelo, Guernica, *All Quiet on the Western Front, Johnny Got His Gun,* war poetry, poster art

THE TRIAL

Strategy: Point–counterpoint

Topic: Art determines society; society determines art.

Skill: Argumentation, research, writing

Concept: Art and literature are records of history.

Fact: History books, photography, murals

THEORY (STUDENT CREATED)

Theory 1: Art and literature mirror the society that creates them.

Theory 2: An evaluation and analysis of contemporary art and literature reveal the excesses and empire building of today's society.

Time Frame: Two weeks

Course: World History

Notes: Like many of the theory building activities, this summarizes well.

INTERVIEW

Strategy: Documentary on early humans

Topic: Cave dwellers

Skill: Research, creating historical personae, videotaping, scripting, sequencing, discrimination of material

Concept: Early humans banded together for the common good.

Fact: Cro-Magnons, Neanderthals

DEMONSTRATION

Strategy: Time lines

Topic: The Great Civilizations: early humans; the Egyptians, the Greeks, the Romans, Great Britain, the United States

Skills: Research, building time lines

Concept: All great civilizations run a cycle.

Fact: The Egyptian, the Greek, the Roman civilizations, and the British Empire have seen their power wane over time.

THE TRIAL

Strategy: Point–counterpoint

Topic: The United States is in the empire stage of the cycle.

Skill: Research, inferential thinking, debate, argumentation

Concept: Empire

Fact: Criteria for an empire, extremes of wealth and poverty, excess in arts and culture, militarism

THEORY (STUDENT CREATED)

Theory 1: Great civilizations follow a cyclical pattern.

Theory 2: The United States is in a phase of world power and dominance.

Time Frame: One week

Course: World History/American Studies

Notes: Again this is a powerful summarizer for a year's activity. However, it can be completed at various other times during the year on a smaller scale. An ideal time is at the completion of the unit on Rome. Comparisons of the Roman Empire and the United States are interesting motivators for students. This exercise powerfully keeps the ideas and lessons from history foremost in students' minds.

INTERVIEW

Strategy: Thought question: Can there be justification used as a defense for committing a crime?

Topic: Bill of Rights

Skill: Interviewing, critical thinking, processing information, reporting

Concept: Our legal system allows for some crimes to be seen as "justified."

Fact: The types of defenses allowed by our legal system

DEMONSTRATION

Strategy: Advertisements (political) in favor of or against limiting the types of defenses allowed by our legal system

Topic: Defendants' rights

Skill: Researching, production of advertisements, creating an argument

Concept: Defendants are guaranteed certain right under the Constitution.

Fact: The amendments framing the Bill of Rights

THE TRIAL

Strategy: Mock trial: The Trial of Goldi Locks

Topic: Trial process, right of the accused, burden of proof charged to the State

Skill: Building and arguing a case for presentation

Concept: A trial is the process used to "get at the truth."

Fact: The stages involved in creating and presenting a criminal case

THEORY (STUDENT CREATED)

Theory 1: Crimes can not be justified in a universal system of law.

Theory 2: There is justification for committing certain crimes. Each case is a separate entity.

Time Frame: Unit

Course: Law/Civics

Notes: This unit would extend to six to eight weeks, though it could be shortened. Theory building would take place at the end of the unit and could be done at the individual or group levels.

INTERVIEW

Strategy: Interview (interviews with ten students representing people involved in some way, directly or indirectly, with the attack on Pearl Harbor. These would include four from the United States, two from Japan, two from the United Kingdom, and two from the Soviet Union).

Topic: Attack on Pearl Harbor

Skill: Researching, interviewing, critical thinking, presentation of data

Concept: Individuals from different nations had different motives and interpretations of the significance of the attack on Pearl Harbor.

Fact: Actions on December 7, 1941 brought the United States directly into World War II.

DEMONSTRATION

Strategy: Maps and time lines

Topic: Movements of the Japanese and American military (naval) forces and diplomatic encounters during the month preceding the attack on Pearl Harbor.

Skills: Researching, map making, presentation of data gained

Concept: The Japanese attack came as part of a coordinated effort between segments of the Japanese government.

Fact: Military and diplomatic actions were taking place during the month preceding the attack.

THE TRIAL

Strategy: Historical trial: Trial of leader(s) from the United Kingdom or Soviet Union for having prior knowledge of the attack on Pearl Harbor but failing to warn the United States

Topic: Attack on Pearl Harbor

Skill: Presenting a case

Concept: Other governments, later our "allies," had motives for helping the United States enter the war.

Fact: Some records throw suspicion on our allies for having prior information indicating an attack yet not sharing that information with the United States.

THEORY (STUDENT CREATED)

Theory 1: The Soviet Union and United Kingdom needed the United States to become involved in World War II.

Theory 2: The attack on Pearl Harbor was only known about ahead of time by the Japanese.

Time Frame: Four weeks

Course: American History/World History

Notes: Students should be allowed ample time to create personae from the research literature.

INTERVIEW

Strategy: News report. Subject: settlement patterns

Topic: Settlement in early New England

Skill: Research, reporting, videography

Concept: Settlement of New England was influenced by physical geography.

Fact: Geography and physical features slowed east-west settlement of New England.

DEMONSTRATION

Strategy: Map of New England demonstrating travel and transportation patterns today

Topic: Geography and travel

Skills: Researching, cartography, assimilation of travel and transportation patterns into maps

Concept: Travel today is influenced by geographical features.

Fact: Travel today remains according to river valley formations rather than according to area needs.

THE TRIAL

Strategy: Debate

Topic: The feasibility of linking Maine with northern Vermont by building an interstate highway.

Skill: Debate, research

Concept: Natural features impact cost effectiveness.

Fact: There is no major highway link in this area.

THEORY (STUDENT CREATED)

Theory 1: Geography must be taken into account in understanding the travel and transportation patterns of an area.

Theory 2: Technology can compensate for physical geography in shaping the transportation patterns of an area.

Time Frame: Two weeks

Course: 8th grade Geography

Notes: This activity can be extended by incorporating the current efforts at providing transportation to this region. This strategy can fit any area of the United States.

INTERVIEW

Strategy: Thought question: Did you gain economically during the 1980s?

Topic: Domestic economics

Skill: Interviewing and reporting

Concept: The effect of the growth of an economy in a democratic society

Fact: Personal wealth increased during the 1980s

DEMONSTRATION

Strategy: Chart

Topic: Stock market/Dow Jones averages during the 1980s

Skills: Researching, creating charts, explaining charts

Concept: Government policy has an effect on the stock market.

Fact: The Dow Jones averages rose during the 1980s.

THE TRIAL

Strategy: Point–counterpoint: The economic policies of the 1980s distributed wealth evenly.

Topic: Economics of the 1980s

Skill: Researching and reporting, critical thinking, evaluation, presenting an argument

Concept: The effect of government policy on the distribution of wealth

Fact: The distribution of personal and corporate wealth during the 1980s

THEORY (STUDENT CREATED)

Theory 1: The economic policies of the 1980s increased class distinctions.

Theory 2: The economic policies of the 1980s distributed the wealth of the 1980s more evenly than the previous policies had.

Time Frame: Two weeks

Course: American Government/Civics

Notes: This activity can be (and has been) used with students in grades 8 through 12 studying Government and Economics. Amending for different age groups is possible.

INTERVIEW

Strategy: Interview (students interview students representing members of various Native American tribes).

Topic: Forced movements of tribes from native homelands

Skill: Research, presentation of information

Concept: Native Americans were seen as a threat to existing and expanding white European society.

Fact: Native American tribes lost land to white settlers.

DEMONSTRATION

Strategy: Map/time lines of forced movement of particular tribes

Topic: Forced movements of tribes from native homelands and white European expansion across the continent

Skill: Research, constructing a time line, cartography

Concept: The concept of personal "ownership" of tracts of land was a point of contention between whites and natives, the use of "law" and government force to move native tribes

Fact: Particular tribes lost land at particular times.

THE TRIAL

Strategy: Historical trial of Andrew Jackson

Topic: Trail of Tears

Skill: Case preparation and presentation

Concept: Government policy can become a policy of ethnic "movement and/or cleansing."

Fact: The Cherokee Nation was forcibly moved from their native homelands to what is now Oklahoma.

THEORY (STUDENT CREATED)

Theory 1: Native Americans were victims of ethnic cleansing and removal.

Theory 2: Success of white European society envisioned by the settlers and the United States Government depended on the opening up of Native lands.

Time Frame: Two to four weeks

Course: American Studies, U.S. History

Notes: This set of strategies can be modified to work with classes that range from the early grades to the later grades.

CHAPTER 7

Conclusion

These strategies and activities are a starting point for the classroom teacher to build a curriculum that addresses the needs of a society entering the twenty-first century. We have presented building blocks that are open to modification and flexible enough to allow for teacher creativity, to enfranchise an increasingly diverse student body.

A NOTE ABOUT DIVERSITY

Society continues to grow more and more diverse. Recognizing and respecting that sense of diversity in cultures and in lifestyles is important if any society is to survive. Rather than exclude diversity and limit the scope to be learned in the social studies classroom, these strategies capitalize on the diversity inherent in our society, a diversity of thought, a diversity of lifestyle, and a diversity of cultures. Yet, for any society to survive, there needs to be a unifying set of principles and mores that establishes some sense of common ground for everyone. People, all people, must feel that they are meaningful and positive participants in society. To accomplish this we need to think of schooling (especially the social studies) as a force that celebrates diversity, fosters tolerance, and encourages the development of a sense of community.

The recognition of the diversity and commonality we share should encourage us to share the strengths that each of us possesses to assist others. We believe that, although some students are better readers than others are, there are nonreaders who, once presented with the information and the process, are effective at organization, leadership, and creative and critical insight. Similarly, some students develop admirable study and homework habits and others never do. Cooperative work uses the individuals' strengths in one area to help better their skills in another.

The strategies we have presented encourage students to look at the diversity that comes from ideas and cultures. If we expect our students to develop a variety of ideas and sound opinions at the end of an educational experience, then we must require our students to work together as they explore and exchange ideas. To this end, our strategies advocate that students recognize the importance of sharing the diversity of their ideas as they work together toward a common goal.

ACCOUNTABILITY

Kerry offered one of the best summaries of education during the past two decades as we worked on this manuscript. He believed that during the 1970s we adopted a student-centered curriculum across the nation that, though celebrating student potential, ignored student accountability and responsibility. During the 1980s and early 1990s, the cycle has reversed as *accountability* and *standards* have become the latest educational buzzwords. In many ways the strategies in this manuscript seek to address both issues. We *can have fun* in the classroom while still holding students accountable to a fair and recognizable set of standards. This is especially effective when students have a sense of input that leads to ownership of those standards. But lessons and strategies can only go so far. Our hope is that they serve as catalysts in positively affecting other issues, such as behavior, attendance, and class participation. To this goal we have structured our evaluations to hold students accountable and responsible in both the cognitive and affective domains.

INTEGRATING STUDENT LEARNING

Our strategies integrate the material and ideas contained in the social studies class with the real-life world of a student. They seek to allow students to see the importance of a way of life, an issue, or an idea as significant to their own lives.

The relevance of social studies should not be removed from the world of students. It must become part of their lives. The same should be true in every area of learning we encounter in formal schooling. If we are to demand that schools get the best from students, we need to look seriously at what schools are giving students. In particular, we must recognize that students gain personal meaning from the material. The material we cover in our classes cannot be a detached piece of information that has no other connection than a test question.

It is a crucial mistake to act as if we are on a higher plane than our students. Yes, we are super-ordinate, and we must be in that relationship. We are not equals, nor should we be. But our status is based on our talents of offering direction while we assist in the process of discovery. We are professional guides. In this way discovery brings meaning to learning, a meaning that will have much more significance than a bit of information handed down from the sage on the stage.

We also need to recognize the age factor. Certain age groups respond better to a variety of stimuli and activity. Although the same concepts and facts can be taught to eighth graders and eleventh graders, the nature of the activity that drives the lesson and the level of skill development necessary to produce a final product are far different. The lessons we have presented offer examples that encourage teachers to modify their lessons so students of any age can shape and construct meaning from what they learn through the process of discovery.

THE ELEMENTS OF A LESSON

Each of our lessons focuses on the three important and integral components that frame what we teach. Consequently, we must recognize the inherent nature of what we intend to teach. Identifying these components allows us to come to a greater understanding about what we teach, how we teach, and the perspectives of the students. Students need to discover and master *facts, concepts,* and *skills,* the learning blocks of every successful lesson. If these elements are foremost in every lesson, then this is not just another model to be read and discarded, but a legitimate means for teachers and students to assess and evaluate activity and progress, individually and collectively, within the class.

FINAL THOUGHTS

This collaborative work has been a unique experience for two teachers from separate and distinct backgrounds. We have had the opportunity of sharing the fun that comes from working together, modeling our own examples. As a result of this cooperation, we feel even more strongly now about the positive, supportive, and harmonious instructional benefits of group efforts. We stayed on task (although occasionally we allowed ourselves the luxury of a coffee or soda), were accountable, had fun, and even finished on time.

In conclusion, we hope this book is a beginning in leading other teachers to develop their own work from our proposals. We understand that many of the strategies we have suggested involve a restructuring of the school day. We join you in demanding that there be administrative support for developing new and creative teaching and learning strategies. As teachers, we have seen too many valid and worthwhile projects die because of organizational constraints.

However, the strength of schooling is still what occurs in the classroom. The exchange between student and teacher frames the centerpiece of the process. We also understand that what takes place between students and between teachers is the ultimate hope for education.

It has been our pleasure to create something that is from teachers for teachers and their students.

Bibliography

Berger, P. L., & Luckman, T. (1967). *The social construction of reality*. New York: Anchor Books.

Beyer, B. K. (1971). A concept of decision making. In B. K. Beyer & A. N. Penna (Eds.), *Concepts in the social studies* (pp. 8–10). Washington, DC: National Council for the Social Studies Bulletin 45.

Bloom, B. S. et al. (1956). *Taxonomy of educational objectives. Handbook I: Cognitive domain*. New York: David McKay Co.

Brandwein, P. F. (1971). Concept as ordering. In B. K. Beyer & A. N. Penna (Eds.), *Concepts in the social studies* (pp. 30–33). Washington, DC: National Council for the Social Studies Bulletin 45.

Chapin, J. R., & Gross, R. E. (1973). *Teaching social studies skills*. Boston: Little, Brown & Company.

David, J. L. (1991, May). What it takes to restructure education. *Educational Leadership, 48* (8), pp. 11–15.

Dewey, J. (1958). *Democracy and education*. New York: Macmillian.

Ekland Shoemaker, B. J. (1989, October). Integrative education: A curriculum for the twenty-first century. *Oregon School Study Council, 33* (2), pp. 1–46.

Evans, D. L. (1991, May). The realities of untracking a high school. *Educational Leadership, 48* (8), 16–17.

Fancett, V. S. (1971). Social science concepts and the classroom. In B. K. Beyer & A. N. Penna (Eds.), *Concepts in the social studies* (pp. 4–16). Washington, DC: National Council for the Social Studies Bulletin 45.

Fullan, M. (1991). *The new meaning of educational change*. New York: Teachers College Press.

George, P. S. (1987). *What's the truth about tracking and ability grouping really???* Gainesville, FL: Teacher Education Resource.

Glazer, S. (1990, December). Why schools still have tracking. *Congressional Quarterly's Editorial Research Reports, 1* (48), pp. 746–758.

Glickman, C. (1991, May). Pretending not to know what we know. *Educational Leadership, 48* (8), pp. 4–10.

Goodlad, J. (1984). *A place called school.* New York: McGraw Hill.

Johnson, D., & Johnson, R. (1975). *Learning together and alone.* Englewood Cliffs, NJ: Prentice-Hall.

Joyce, B., & Weil, M. (1980). *Models of teaching (2d ed.).* Englewood Cliffs, NJ: Prentice-Hall.

Kagan, S. (1990). *Cooperative learning: Resources for teachers.* San Juan Capistrano, CA: Resoures for Teachers.

Mead, G. H. (1932 & 1969). *Mind, self, and society.* Chicago: University of Chicago Press.

Nowicki, J. J. (1990, Fall). Teaching in the heterogeneous classroom. *Pioneer Practitioner, 1* (1), pp. 14–16.

Nowicki, J. J. (1991a, Spring). Students respond to detracking: A small scale study. *Pioneer Practitioner, 2* (1), pp. 22–24.

Nowicki, J. J. (1991b, Fall). Toward heterogeneous grouping: Ideas thoughts, insights. *Pioneer Practitioner, 2* (2), pp. 17–20.

Nowicki, J. J. (1992). *A school as a crucible of change: A case study of restructuring and a faculty's culture.* Doctoral Dissertation, University of Massachusetts at Amherst, Amherst, MA.

Nowicki, J. J. (1993, April 29). Students respond to detracking: A small scale study. Paper presented at New England Educational Research Organization Annual Meeting, Portsmouth, NH.

Oakes, J. (1985). *Keeping track: How schools structure inequality.* New Haven, CT: Yale University Press.

Oakes, J. (1986, September). Keeping track, Part 1: The policy and practice of curriculum inequality. *Phi Delta Kappan,* pp. 12–17.

Oakes, J., & Lipton, M. (1990). *Making the best of schools.* New Haven, CT: Yale University Press.

Oakes, J., & Lipton, M. (1992, February). Detracking schools: Early lessons from the field. *Phi Delta Kappan,* pp. 448–454.

Phillips, D. C., & Soltis, J. F. (1991). *Perspectives on learning (2nd Ed.).* New York: Teachers College Press.

Piaget, J. (1969). *Psychology of intelligence.* Patterson, NJ: Littlefield, Adams.

Slavin, R. (1980). Cooperative learning. *Review of Educational Research, 50,* pp. 315–342.

Slavin, R. (1983). *Cooperative learning.* New York: Longman.

Slavin, R. (1987). Ability grouping and student achievement in elementary schools: A best-evidence synthesis. *Review of Educational Research, 57* (3), 293–336.

Slavin, R. (1988). Synthesis of research on grouping in elementary and secondary schools. *Educational Leadership, 46* (9), pp. 67–77.

Slavin, R. E. (1989). *School and classroom organization.* Hillsdale, NJ: Lawrence Erlbaum Associates.

Slavin, R. (1990). Achievement effects of ability grouping in secondary schools: A best-evidence synthesis. *Review of Educational Research, 60* (3), pp. 471–499.

Solas, J. (1992, Summer). Investigating teacher and student thinking about the process of teaching and learning using autobiography and pepetory grid. *Review of Educational Research, 62* (2), pp. 205–225.

Taba, H. (1967). *Teachers handbook for elementary social studies.* Palo Alto: Addison-Wesley.

Tanck, M. L. (1969). Teaching concepts, generalizations, and constructs. In D. McClure Fraser (Ed.): *Social studies curriculum development: Prospects and problems* (pp. 100–139). Washington, DC: NCSS 39th Yearbook.

Tyrrel, R. (1990, January). What teachers say about cooperative learning. *Middle School Journal, 21* (3), pp. 16–19.

Veves, M. (1989, Fall). Beyond tracking: A teacher's view. *Equity and Choice,* pp. 18–22.

Wheelock, A. (1992). *Crossing the tracks: How untracking can save America's schools.* New York: The New Press.

Appendix

INTERVIEW STRATEGIES

Course:

Length of Activity:

Grade Level:

Unit:

Topic:

Title:

Description of Activity: (Circle one)

Documentary   News Report   Interview   Thought Question

Overview:

Number of Students:

List of Roles:

Concepts:

**Factual
Information:**

Skills:

**Time Table of
Activities:**

TIME FRAME (BY WEEK/BY DAY)

(   )
(   )
(   )
(   )
(   )
(   )
(   )
(   )

Evaluation:

**Corollaries to
Murphy's Law:**

INTERVIEW—STUDENT EVALUATION FORM

Name: _____

Activity/Date: _____

Time Period: _____

My Role Was: _____

What New
Information
Did I Learn? _____

_____

_____

_____

_____

The Resources
I Used Were:

Printed Word: _____

_____

_____

Other Sources: _____

_____

_____

_____

Peer Evaluator: _____

Evaluator's
Comments: _____

_____

_____

_____

_____

DEMONSTRATION STRATEGIES

Course:

Length of Activity:

Grade Level:

Unit:

Topic:

Title:

**Description of
Activity:**

Overview:

**Number of
Students:**

Concepts:

**Factual
Information:**

Skills:

Time Table of
Activities:

TIME FRAME (BY WEEK/BY DAY)

(   )
(   )
(   )
(   )
(   )
(   )
(   )
(   )

Evaluation:

Corollaries to
Murphy's Law:

DEMONSTRATION BIBLIOGRAPHY FORM

MID EAST DAY FORM 1

Your Name Is _____

Welcome to the Mid East Day assignment. Please do not lose this piece of paper as it contains your instructions and is a place for you to list important information as you go along. Please be kind enough to show this note to your parents.

As you know, we (all seventh graders) will be displaying presentations about the Mid East–North Africa region of the world one day during the last part of January. In this presentation you will be required to demonstrate the knowledge you have gained about a particular topic of life in the Middle East or North Africa. Topics are of your own choice. Your presentation will be evaluated by teachers and shared with other students, parents, and faculty on Mid East Day. Presentations should include (but are not limited to) clothing to support your presentation, visual displays, cultural artifacts, food where applicable, charts, maps, graphs, and whatever else you find helpful. You will be required to turn in a formal bibliography and a short written statement that talks about what you learned from your project and what you learned from the process of putting together your presentation. While this is a very serious and important component of this quarter's grade, it is also an activity that can be a lot of *fun*. Be as creative as you can!

REQUIRED RESEARCH (MINIMUM REQUIREMENTS)

You must have at least seven references from books; six from magazine articles; and seven from other sources such as encyclopedias and other reference material. You must list the source and page number along with other bibliographical information where possible. Use the chart that follows to help you organize your presentation and the sources of information that you will use. Enter the dates that you found the information.

Topic: _____ Date Selected _____

Book References:

Date _____ Source_____ Pg _____

Date _____ Source_____ Pg _____

Date _____ Source_____ Pg _____

Date _____ Source_____ Pg _____

Date _____ Source_____ Pg _____

Date _____ Source_____ Pg _____

Date _____ Source_____ Pg _____

Magazine or Journal Articles:

Date _____ Source _____ Pg _____

Date _____ Source _____ Pg _____

Date _____ Source _____ Pg _____

Date _____ Source _____ Pg _____

Date _____ Source _____ Pg _____

Date _____ Source _____ Pg _____

Date _____ Source _____ Pg _____

Other Reference Sources: (pages where applicable)

Date _____ Source _____ Pg _____

Date _____ Source _____ Pg _____

Date _____ Source _____ Pg _____

Date _____ Source _____ Pg _____

Date _____ Source _____ Pg _____

Date _____ Source _____ Pg _____

Date _____ Source _____ Pg _____

This form should be completed in two weeks and will be updated as information gathering continues.

STUDENT PROGRESS OUTLINE

Mid East Day Form 2

Date _____

Your Name Is _____

As Mid East Day draws near and as we begin to conclude the research and preparation that began during the first week of the term, it is now time to outline the presentations that you will make as part of the Mid East Day experience. This form assumes that you will be presenting along the lines of the topic and 20 research sources you listed on Mid East Day Form 1.

Please identify and describe five (5) *separate* parts to your Mid East Day presentation with at least one sentence. These five (5) parts represent the minimum requirements in grading.

Part 1 _____

_____

_____

Part 2 _____

_____

_____

Part 3 _____

_____

_____

Part 4 _____

_____

_____

Part 5 _____

_____

_____

Please describe the costume that you will wear to help you with your presentation.

_____

_____

_____

DEMONSTRATION EVALUATION FORM

(to be used by volunteer teacher evaluating student work)

Student Name: _____

Teacher-Evaluator: _____

Date: _____

Please rate each category from 1 to 5, with 5 signifying exceptional work.

1. Student verbal knowledge of topic

    1   2   3   4   5

2. Quality and detail of visual student demonstration material

    1   2   3   4   5

3. Quality and appropriateness of student costume

    1   2   3   4   5

4. Quality and knowledge of topic demonstrated by written material

    1   2   3   4   5

5. Overall assessment of student presentation

    1   2   3   4   5

DEMONSTRATION EVALUATION FORM

(to be used by student evaluating peer demonstrations work)

Student Name: _____

Student Evaluator: _____

Date: _____

Please rate each category from 1 to 5, with 5 signifying exceptional work.

1. Student verbal knowledge of topic

    1   2   3   4   5

2. Quality and detail of visual student demonstration material

    1   2   3   4   5

3. Quality and appropriateness of student costume

    1   2   3   4   5

4. Quality and knowledge of topic demonstrated by written material

    1   2   3   4   5

5. Overall assessment of student presentation

    1   2   3   4   5

TRIAL STRATEGIES

Type of Activity:

Unit:

Grade:

Title:

**Number of
Students:**

Overview:

Concepts:

Facts:

Skills:

Time:

Evaluation:

**Age/Grade
Expectations:**

**Corollaries to
Murphy's Law:**

THEORY STRATEGY GUIDE

INTERVIEW

Strategy:

Topic:

Skill:

Concept:

Fact:

DEMONSTRATION

Strategy:

Topic:

Concept:

Fact:

THE TRIAL

Strategy:

Topic:

Skill:

Concept:

Fact:

THEORY (STUDENT CREATED)

Theory 1:

Theory 2:

Time Frame:

Course:

Notes:

Index

The Collaborative Social Studies Classroom

A Resource for Teachers, Grades 7–12

Social studies teachers will find dozens of ways to energize their classes using the dynamic classroom strategies presented here. More than 100 sample activities are included—each designed to offer cooperative learning opportunities for students in today's mixed-ability classrooms. These hands-on, student-tested strategies are ready to implement immediately—or they may be modified to suit individual classroom needs.

Each sample lesson describes the factual knowledge, conceptual knowledge, and skills that students are responsible for learning, and suggests specific strategies for evaluating student performance. The sample lessons range in length from a day to a week to a complete unit; many include suggestions for large-group, small-group, and home- or community-based activities. The strategies are designed to help students master the important facts required by the curriculum while developing higher-level thinking skills such as comprehension, application, analysis, synthesis, and evaluation.

High-interest activities include four types of interview strategies, eight types of demonstration activities, four types of trial strategies, and numerous theory-building strategies. Sample activities range from documentary projects and news reports to interviews with family or community members, museum exhibits, map making, time lines, group debates, and mock trials. Examples include a Mideast Day exhibit, the trial of Brutus for the murder of Julius Caesar, a Constitutional Convention debate, making maps of Europe before and after World War I, and a presentation of "My Life as an Early Hunter/Gatherer."

About the Authors

Joseph John Nowicki teaches social studies at Pioneer Valley Regional School in Northfield, Massachusetts, which moved to a nontracked curriculum nearly ten years ago. He is also a lecturer in the Division of Continuing Education and an Adjunct Assistant Professor in the Graduate School of Education at the University of Massachusetts at Amherst.

Kerry F. Meehan has taught junior high, middle school, and high school English, as well as high school social studies and adult education. He currently teaches English and social studies at Pioneer Valley Regional School in Northfield, Massachusetts. For five years he was an assistant principal of Gateway Regional High School, where he was active in curriculum planning.

Longwood Division
Allyn and Bacon
160 Gould Street
Needham Heights, MA 02194-2310

ISBN 0-205-17391-8
H73919

9 780205 173914
90000>

Cover Photograph © Will Faller